HOW TO SECURE YOUR H-1B VISA

A PRACTICAL GUIDE FOR INTERNATIONAL PROFESSIONALS AND THEIR US EMPLOYERS

James A. Bach
Robert G. Werner

Apress®

How to Secure Your H-1B Visa: A Practical Guide for International Professionals and Their US Employers

ISBN-13 (pbk): 978-1-4302-4728-9
ISBN-13 (electronic): 978-1-4302-4729-6

Trademarked names may appear in this book. Rather than use a trademark symbol with every occurrence of a trademarked name, we use the names only in an editorial fashion and to the benefit of the trademark owner, with no intention of infringement of the trademark.

Chair and User navigation icons courtesy of www.visualpharm.com under Creative Commons Attribution-No Derivative Works 3.0 Unported License.

President and Publisher: Paul Manning
Acquisitions Editor: Robert Hutchinson
Editorial Board: Steve Anglin, Mark Beckner, Ewan Buckingham, Gary Cornell, Louise Corrigan, Morgan Ertel, Jonathan Gennick, Jonathan Hassell, Robert Hutchinson, Michelle Lowman, James Markham, Matthew Moodie, Jeff Olson, Jeffrey Pepper, Douglas Pundick, Ben Renow-Clarke, Dominic Shakeshaft, Gwenan Spearing, Matt Wade, Tom Welsh
Coordinating Editor: Rita Fernando
Copy Editor: Tamsin Willard
Compositor: Bytheway Publishing Services
Indexer: SPi Global
Cover Designer: Anna Ischenko

Distributed to the book trade worldwide by Springer-Verlag New York, Inc., 233 Spring Street, 6th Floor, New York, NY 10013. Phone 1-800-SPRINGER, fax 201-348-4505, e-mail orders-ny@springer-sbm.com, or visit www.springeronline.com.

For information on translations, please contact us by e-mail at info@apress.com, or visit www.apress.com.

Apress and friends of ED books may be purchased in bulk for academic, corporate, or promotional use. eBook versions and licenses are also available for most titles. For more information, reference our Special Bulk Sales–eBook Licensing web page at www.apress.com/bulk-sales. To place an order, email your request to support@apress.com

To our wives, Sharon and Siew, for their loving support, patient forbearance, and amiable company during the writing of this book.

Contents

About the Authors

James A. Bach is an immigration attorney in San Francisco. He has been working exclusively with immigration cases for several decades, and has lectured and written extensively on immigration law subjects. He currently serves as Commissioner on the California State Bar's Immigration and Nationality Advisory Commission, which writes and grades the California Immigration and Nationality Specialty Examination, and was past Chair of the Commission. He was one of the first Legal Specialists in Immigration and Nationality Law certified by the State Bar of California Board of Legal Specialization. He received a JD from Hastings College of the Law, University of California, and a BA from Dartmouth College.

Robert G. Werner has been practicing immigration law in San Francisco since 1971 and has been certified as a Legal Specialist in Immigration and Nationality Law by the State Bar of California Board of Legal Specialization for over 20 years. As a commissioner of the California State Bar Immigration and Nationality Advisory Commission, he contributed to the writing and grading of the immigration specialty exam. He received a JD from Boalt Hall School of Law, University of California, where he was Book Review Editor of the Law Review and graduated in the top tenth of his class, and he took a BA with honors from Harvard College.

Acknowledgments

We acknowledge and thank the American Immigration Lawyers Association (AILA) and its extraordinary efforts over many decades in compiling most of the documents that appear in the appendices of the present work.

Introduction

With a combined 60 years of experience handling H-1B visas, we have worked with hundreds of employers and thousands of H-1B professionals. These thousands of H-1B cases have brought benefits to all concerned. Employers are able to find the best and brightest workers from a potential applicant pool of 7 billion people (the population of the world) instead of 312 million (the population of the United States, representing less than 5% of the world's population). The United States is revitalized through the presence of hard-working, law-abiding, highly educated, and very smart immigrants. And immigrants are able to share the wonderful gift of living in America: a place of prosperity, civil order, justice, freedom, beauty, and integrity.

US immigration laws do not allow everyone who wants to live in America to do so, but they do provide for temporary and permanent residence in the United States for the best and the brightest scientists, engineers, professors, physicians, researchers, and other professionals. And the H-1B visa is the gateway.

We have written this book with several purposes in mind:

- To provide a guide through the maze of H-1B laws and policies

- To help you ensure the success of your application, from H-1B petition to visa issuance

- To help you avoid the pitfalls, liabilities, and disasters that are sometimes associated with H-1B status

This book is written for both H-1B employers and H-1B employees. When we use the term "you," we are addressing both employers and employees, except where navigation icons (see key below) indicate that a given section preferentially addresses one rather than the other.

Navigation Key   To assist you in navigating through the book, we mark chapter titles and section headings as follows:

   Sections that might be of more interest to *employers* have an icon of an empty chair to be filled by an H-1B employee!

   Sections that are directed mostly to *employees* have an icon of the H-1B employee with his passport out, waiting to be stamped with an H-1B visa.

    Sections that equally concern *both employers and employees* have both icons.

What Is an H-1B Visa?

An H-1B visa provides the authorization for foreign professionals to work for certain employers in the United States for six years (and even longer). The initial H-1B visa normally is issued for three years; the H-1B status can then be extended for at least another three years. Those with H-1B visas can travel freely into and out of the United States, but they can work only for employers who have submitted H-1B petitions for them.

Most H-1B workers are engineers, IT workers, scientists, and teachers, but anyone with a bachelor's degree (or equivalent education and experience) may be eligible for H-1B status. H-1B visas have been granted to a wide range of professionals, including accountants, medical technologists, logistics experts, business managers, statisticians, doctors, nurses, and marketing professionals.

There are three basic requirements for H-1B eligibility:

- The worker must have a bachelor's degree in a specialty field (or equivalent training and experience).

- The job normally must require that degree.

- The employer must pay the H-1B employee a salary that is consistent with the average salaries paid for the occupation and consistent with the salaries paid to other workers in the company.

There are many other types of temporary ("nonimmigrant") visas, as well as a permanent visa (called a "green card" or "immigrant" visa). The H-1B visa has many advantages over these other types of visas for both employers and employees.

Advantages and Disadvantages of H-1B Status for Employers

For employers, the *advantages* of H-1B status over other types of visas include the following:

- **Certainty.** For most scientific, engineering, teaching, and IT positions, the H-1B petition is typically successful.

- **Speed.** Often a new H-1B visa can be obtained within a month or so of the job offer. Employees who are already in the United States in H-1B status can often begin the employment within a week or two of the offer.

- **Longevity.** Professionals can work in H-1B status for up to six years, and indefinitely if the green card application process is started by the end of their fifth year.

For employers, the *disadvantages* of H-1B status compared with other types of visas include the following:

- **Quota restrictions.** One disadvantage of the H-1B visa is that it is not available at certain times of the year when the annual quota has been filled. However, that quota does not apply to those who have already been granted H-1B status, and many employers, such as universities, are exempt from the quota.

- **Labor cost.** The H-1B visa is a way to recruit and secure the best and brightest employees and to be more competitive, not a way to save money immediately. In fact, employers often pay their H-1B employees more than they pay their other workers, because they are more qualified. As discussed in Chapter 8, the Department of Labor has devised an elaborate (and often perplexing) system to ensure that H-1B employees are not underpaid.

- **Fees.** The employer must pay certain upfront costs to get the H-1B visa. Those costs, which involve a combination of filing fees and legal fees, normally total between $4,000 and $6,000 (depending on several factors, including the size of the company, whether it is the first H-1B petition, whether "Premium Processing" is used, and the legal fee charged by the attorney).

- **Liability to penalties.** Another disadvantage for employers is the liability for fines and other penalties if the H-1B worker is underpaid or if the employer fails to follow formal requirements for ensuring a competitive salary. However, employers can avoid those fines and penalties by carefully following the guidance in this book and the advice of their immigration attorneys. In Chapter 8, we will discuss in detail how employers can comply with the H-1B requirements to avoid fines and penalties.

- There may be alternatives to H-1B status, summarized in Chapter 12, if any of these restrictions prevent or delay H-1B status.

Benefits and Challenges of H-1B Status for Employees

For the H-1B employee, the *advantages* of H-1B status include the following:

- **Predictability.** You are assured of being able to work and live in the United States for six years or longer, as long as you keep your H-1B employment.

- **Portability.** You can easily transfer from one employer to another.

- **Ability to immigrate.** An intent to later immigrate to the United States (i.e., get a "green card") does not invalidate your H-1B visa or create problems in getting it. In contrast, most other nonimmigrant visas (for example, a student visa) require evidence that you intend to return to your home country and have no intention to immigrate.

There are some *disadvantages* to life in the United States in H-1B status, and those should be considered before you make the decision to emigrate from your home country:

- **Spouse work restrictions.** Spouses of those in H-1B status are not authorized to work in the United States unless they can independently qualify for H-1B or another visa status. However, they are eligible to attend college or pursue other education such as English or cooking classes. Most H-1B employees are young (in their 20s and 30s), and many spouses spend their time taking care of children—often a full-time job!

- **Work relocation restrictions.** A new application must be filed each time the employee changes jobs and each time the work location changes. That makes it cumbersome not only to change employers but also to change job locations with the same employer. In Chapter 8 we will discuss the requirements for changing job locations, which can be particularly challenging for the traveling consultant. Those considerations, however, are primarily the employer's concern.

- Other than these restrictions, a person in H-1B status has almost all of the rights and freedoms of US permanent residents. They can pursue their careers, travel abroad, and even purchase a home.

Chapter Takeaway   The H-1B program helps US employers to become more productive, innovative, and competitive. It enables highly skilled professionals to live and work in the United States and can be a first step to later US permanent residence.

Overview of the H-1B Petition Procedure

The H-1B petition can be prepared as soon as the prospective employee[1] has accepted a job offer.

US Government Agencies Involved in the H-1B Visa Process

The H-1B visa process normally involves applications to four different US government agencies, in the following order:

1. **US Department of Labor.** The *employer* will file a *Labor Condition Application* (**LCA**)[2] with the US Department of Labor. Approval of the LCA takes approximately one week.

2. **US Citizenship and Immigration Services.** The *employer* will file the **H-1B petition** with US Citizenship and Immigration Services (USCIS). Processing typically takes two weeks or so with "Premium Processing" (discussed in Chapter 6).

---

[1] In this book we use the term *employee* loosely to refer to prospective as well as actual H-1B employees, depending on context.

[2] Not to be confused with a *Labor Certification Application*, used to obtain a green card.

3. **US embassy or consulate.** The *employee* will apply for the **H-1B visa** at a US embassy or US consulate. This process can take from one to six weeks, depending on the backlog at the embassy or consulate.

4. **US Customs and Border Protection.** The *employee* will present the **H-1B visa** at a US port of entry (international airport or land border) to obtain admission into the US.

Not all of these agencies are involved in every H-1B case. For example, someone who is already in H-1B status with another employer may not need to follow the last two steps.

By adding up these various processing times and accounting for the time required to prepare the various applications, we can estimate that the time it takes to obtain an H-1B visa or status ranges from one to two months for an employee who has never been in H-1B status, and from one to two weeks for someone who is already employed in H-1B status by another employer.

US Department of Labor

Historically, the Department of Labor (**DOL**) was not involved in the H-1B visa process. However, in 1998, Congress introduced the Labor Condition Application (LCA), to be issued by the Department of Labor before an H-1B petition could be filed.

Essentially, the LCA was designed to make sure that the H-1B program does not depress the salaries and benefits of American workers. Congress was concerned that the H-1B program was undercutting the salaries of professionals in the US because employers were paying the H-1B employees less than they paid American workers. To address this perceived problem, Congress required all employers filing H-1B petitions to promise to pay any H-1B employee a *competitive salary*.

In the language of the LCA rules, a "competitive salary" has three conceptual components:

>*Actual Wage*: the amount paid by the employer to others with similar experience and qualifications for the specific position.

>*Prevailing Wage*: the weighted average salary for that specific occupational classification paid by all employers in the geographic area of intended employment.

>*Required Wage*: the **higher** of the *Actual Wage* and the *Prevailing Wage*.

The H-1B employer must agree to pay the **Required Wage**. The employer may pay more than the Required Wage, but the LCA and the H-1B petition must indicate the Required Wage, and employers are subject to penalties if they pay less than that.

The role of the DOL is to make sure that employers pay the Required Wage and to investigate and penalize employers who do not. The investigations and prosecutions are led by the *Wage and Hour Division* of the DOL—the same entity that investigates and prosecutes federal minimum wage and overtime violations. The Wage and Hour Division is well funded, with aggressive investigators and attorneys on its staff. Employers are therefore well advised to pay close attention to the LCA requirements. In Chapter 8, we will discuss ways to achieve compliance with those requirements.

The government does not vet the truth of an LCA prior to approval, which is automatic provided all the formal requirements of the LCA filing are met. However, it is subject to a later audit by the DOL, which will assess penalties if the statements on the LCA are not accurate.

There are essentially four statements that the employer must make on the LCA, as follows:

- *The employer will pay the H-1B employee the Required Wage for the entire period of H-1B employment.*

- *The employment of the H-1B worker will not have an adverse impact on the working conditions of other workers.* Examples of factors that could create an adverse impact would be making salaried H-1B employees work longer hours than other employees, or making them travel more.

- *There is no strike or labor dispute in progress.* This is usually not an issue for H-1B employees, who are usually in professions that are not unionized. However, some professional occupations, such as teachers or nurses, might be involved in organized labor disputes.

- *Notice of the LCA was given to the employer's other employees* (normally by posting notices at the place where the H-1B employee will work).

Failure to comply with any of these LCA conditions can subject the employer to monetary and other penalties. In addition, with certain exceptions, failure to file an LCA for *each place* the H-1B employee will work will also subject the employer to penalties.

In sum, the role of the DOL in the H-1B process is to process and approve the LCA, investigate the approved LCAs on a post-audit basis, and conduct civil prosecutions if there are violations.

 ## US Citizenship and Immigration Services

US Citizenship and Immigration Services (**USCIS**) is part of the *US Department of Homeland Security* (DHS). It is the agency that processes and approves applications for immigration benefits, including H-1B petitions. USCIS maintains two different offices on opposite sides of the country, the *Vermont Service Center* (VSC) and the *California Service Center* (CSC), to process H-1B and other employment-based immigration petitions.

Where the employer should file the H-1B petition depends on the location of the proposed employment. Generally, petitions for employment in the eastern half of the United States are filed with the VSC in St. Albans, Vermont, and petitions for employment in the western half of the United States are filed with the CSC in Laguna Niguel, California.

The H-1B petition essentially consists of:

- the filing fee
- the H-1B petition form (Form I-129)
- the approved LCA
- the employer's letter explaining the proposed employment
- evidence of the employee's qualifications and professional background (such as a copy of college degrees and transcripts)

The role of USCIS is to determine whether

- the proposed employment normally requires a specialty college degree or equivalent education and experience
- the employee has that background
- it is likely that the proposed employment will take place as described
- the employer actually exists and can pay the offered salary (that is, whether it is a real job offer and not a fake)

Although those items may appear to be simple to determine, H-1B eligibility can be a complex issue, as we will explain in Chapter 4.

If USCIS determines that the employee and the job will support H-1B status, it will issue an *approval notice* (**I-797**), which it will mail to the employer and the employer's attorney. It will also notify the US State Department of the approval, and provide a copy of the H-1B petition to the State Department via a secure system called **PIMS** (*Petition Information Management System*). The PIMS system is administered by a State Department office, the Kentucky Consular Center (KCC).

 ## US Department of State

The US Department of State (**DOS**), through its worldwide *embassies and consulates*, is responsible for *granting the* **H-1B visa,** which is a *stamp in the employee's passport.* The application for the visa is made directly to the embassy or consulate, which requires the applicant to have an **interview with a consular officer** before the visa can be granted. The embassy or consulate will obtain a copy of the H-1B petition and its approval from the PIMS system.

 Caution   There is no system for alerting the employee, the employer, or the employer's attorney as to whether the H-1B petition approval has been entered in PIMS, so occasionally an employee will apply for the H-1B visa only to find that the PIMS notification was not made. That circumstance results in delays in visa issuance until the problem can be corrected. However, problems with PIMS are becoming increasingly rare, and generally, employees can assume that the *US embassy or consulate has notice of the approval within a week or so of petition approval.*

The application for the H-1B visa by the employee is a separate process from the employer's H-1B petition and normally proceeds without the employer's involvement.

 Exception for India   Consulates in India often require additional documents from the *employer.*

Usually, the H-1B visa applicant will apply at the US consulate or US embassy closest to his or her residence (but that is not always required). The **H-1B visa application** consists of:

- an online application form
- a visa application fee

- a passport-sized photograph that is uploaded with the application

The applicant must also present a *valid and unexpired passport*.

⇨ **Tip**   If your passport will expire soon, we recommend you obtain a new passport before applying for the visa.

Presenting a passport that will not expire for several years is advisable, because US Customs and Border Protection (CBP) inspectors may limit the period of admission in H-1B status to the expiration date of the passport (or the expiration date plus six months). By first securing a passport that will not expire for several years, you can avoid a limited initial admission period that you would be required to extend at a later date.

💣 **Caution**   CBP inspectors are inconsistent in this regard. Sometimes they will limit the period of admission based on the passport expiration date, but often they will admit you for the entire period of your H-1B approval notice (Form I-797), despite an earlier passport expiration date.

The best place to start the visa application process is on the embassy or consulate website. A link to all of the US embassies and consulates in the world can be found at http://www.usembassy.gov/. Once you are on the embassy or consulate website, you will find a link to "Visas," then a further link to "Nonimmigrant visas" that will contain instructions for completing the H-1B visa application.

🏴 **Exception for India**   The US diplomatic posts in India are different from most other US embassies and consulates because they have contracted with a private company, CGI Group Inc., to handle the visa applications (although the consular officers at the embassy or consulates still conduct the interviews). Information and application forms for applying for a US visa in India can be found on the CGI Group website, at http://www.ustraveldocs.com/in.

The **spouse and minor children** of the H-1B employee can obtain **H-4 visas**. You would normally apply for any H-4 visas at the same time as you apply for the H-1B visa, but you do not have to do this. Sometimes the H-1B employee may obtain her visa first, and her family members may apply for their H-4 visas later. Since the H-4 visa is dependent on the H-1B visa, you can never obtain it *before* obtaining the H-1B visa or status.

⇨ **Tip**   Consular officers, especially in India, often prefer that the H-1B and H-4 applications be submitted together.

Before issuing the H-1B visa, the consular officer must make sure that the H-1B employee is **admissible** into the US. Evidence of illegal drug use, even without a criminal conviction, could make you inadmissible. One arrest or conviction for drunk driving during the previous three years, or two drunk-driving arrests or convictions at any time, will require you to be evaluated by a doctor (to determine whether you are inadmissible because of alcoholism, a medical condition) before a visa will be issued.

If you previously violated any immigration law or status, you could be denied a visa. There are many other **grounds of inadmissibility**, as discussed in Chapter 7. If you believe you may be inadmissible, you should discuss the matter with an attorney before applying for the visa.

If there is any doubt as to your admissibility, the embassy or consulate may delay issuing the visa until it conducts a background check. This background check, called **Administrative Processing**, may involve:

- A criminal background check via CIA, FBI, and Interpol databases
- A local investigation using embassy or consulate local resources

Often, Administrative Processing is triggered because:

- The visa applicant has the same name and birth date as a criminal or terrorist
- There is doubt as to whether documents such as college degrees are genuine
- There is doubt as to whether there is a genuine job offer or employer

---

Caution   Although relatively rare, Administrative Processing can upset and delay the plans of both employer and employee for a very long time.

US Customs and Border Protection

The final agency involved in the H-1B process is US Customs and Border Protection (**CBP**). As its name implies, CBP is charged with making sure that only those with the right to do so enter the United States. For most H-1B employees, that means having a *valid, unexpired* **H-1B visa** and a *valid, unexpired* **passport**.

⇨ **Exception for Canada**   The one exception to this rule is that citizens of Canada are not required to have a visa (but they are required to have a valid passport or other acceptable evidence of Canadian citizenship). However, landed immigrants of Canada (those who have the right to live permanently in Canada, but who are not Canadian citizens) *are* required to have a visa.

Upon arrival in the United States, you—the H-1B employee—will present yourself for **inspection** at the *port of entry* (usually the international section of the first airport arrived at in the US, or at a land port if you drive across the border). CBP will inspect your passport, H-1B visa, and a copy of your H-1B approval notice (Form I-797, issued previously by USCIS) and will capture your biometrics (always digital or ink fingerprints and increasingly iris and facial recognition scans, too). CBP will then issue an *Arrival–Departure Record* (**Form I-94**), which will be *stamped by the CBP officer and stapled into the passport*. The I-94 will indicate your date of arrival and the expiration date of your authorized stay in H-1B status.

⇨ **Note**   Form I-94 is a small white card that is attached to the visa page of your passport at the port of entry. Currently, CBP is in the process of eliminating the I-94 and will soon move to an all-electronic entry/departure tracking system.

As noted above, the expiration date of your authorized stay on your I-94 will *usually* be the expiration date of your H-1B approval notice (I-797), which is normally the same date as the expiration date of your H-1B visa, plus 10 days. However, the CBP inspector *might* limit your authorized stay on the I-94 because your passport will expire early or because of an error.

💣 **Caution**   It is prudent to check the expiration date of your Form I-94 immediately when it is issued and challenge the CBP inspector (in a nice way!) if the expiration date appears to be wrong.

⇨ **Preclearance Exceptions**   At certain international airports, CBP inspects H-1B visa holders and other nonimmigrants[3] *before they travel to the United States.* These airports include Heathrow Airport in London and the international airports in Canada and Ireland. A complete list of these "preclearance" airports can be found at http://www.cbp.gov/xp/cgov/toolbox/contacts/preclear_locations.xml.

In addition to determining whether you have the proper documents to enter the US in H-1B status, CBP will, like the US embassy or consulate, make its own determination as to whether you are admissible to the United States. The CBP officer will almost certainly ask you if you intend to work for the H-1B employer named on the H-1B approval notice (Form I-797) or, if you are returning to the US, whether you are still employed with the H-1B sponsor.

The Importance of Being Earnest

As noted in our introduction, American governmental institutions are famous for their integrity, and that is one of the attractions of living and working in the United States. To preserve that integrity, government agencies are strenuously proactive in uncovering fraud or lies in the visa process. In fact, the employer must pay a $500 *fraud fee* with every initial H-1B petition: money that goes into a fund for investigating and prosecuting fraud.

Each stage of the H-1B application process, summarized above, requires **truthful statements** to the various government agencies: **DOL**, **USCIS**, **DOS**, and **CBP**. Failure to be honest in any of the applications has the potential to undermine the H-1B system, and for that reason fraud incurs severe consequences if detected. In Chapter 9, we will detail the penalties both employers and employees face if they are not truthful in the various stages of the H-1B petition procedure.

Chapter Takeaway   *Any sort of dishonesty* could lead both employer and employee to wish that they had never started the H-1B procedure in the first place.

---

[3] A nonimmigrant is a person who is not an immigrant (i.e., who has a temporary visa instead of a green card).

The H-1B Annual Quota

Critical Timing Issues

Congress imposes an annual quota on H-1B visas, which it varies over time. The quota raises critical issues of timing for new H-1B petitions and of eligibility for seven distinct quota exemptions. These issues of timing and eligibility must be weighed jointly and carefully by employees and employers.

Quota History

Because of the perceived threat to American workers, Congress imposed an annual quota on H-1B visas, beginning in 1992 and continuing to the present. This quota was initially set at 65,000 new H-1B visas each year, a level that was maintained from 1992 through 1997. Beginning in 1998, it increased each year, reaching a high point of 195,000 in 2001 before declining to 65,000 in 2004. In 2004, Congress added 20,000 visas to the quota for those who obtain US master's degrees, resulting in the current annual quota of 85,000 H-1B petitions.[1]

The annual quota is based on the US government's fiscal year, which begins October 1 and ends September 30. That is why many H-1B approval notices and visas have a starting date of October 1.

Before 2004, the annual quota of 195,000 was generally sufficient to accommodate the demand for new H-1B visas. However, the reduced quota of 85,000 is oversubscribed each year, with a varying demand that in recent years has exceeded roughly 120,000 per year. Once the quota is filled, many

---

[1] This quota may be increased in 2013.

people who wish to petition for H-1B status must wait until the following fiscal year.

The timing of filing a new H-1B petition is therefore crucial. The government permits the H-1B petition to be filed beginning on April 1—six months before the effective date of the H-1B petition of October 1—and accepts petitions until the quota is filled. In years of high demand, the quota is filled in the first few days that filing is permitted (that is, the first week of April). In low-demand years, it may be several months after April before the quota is filled. Since the quota was reduced in 2004, it has been filled at different times during the months following April 1, as follows:

- 2005   August 10
- 2006   April 1 (July 27 for those with US master's degrees)
- 2007   April 2[2] (April 30 for those with US master's degrees)
- 2008   April 1

"Great Recession" begins

- 2009   December 21
- 2010   January 26, 2011
- 2011   November 22

Partial recovery from the "Great Recession"

- 2012   June 12
- 2013   April 1 (expected)

As you can see, demand for H-1B visas is high when the US economy is strong and the unemployment rate is low (e.g., 2006, 2007, and 2008), and demand is low when the economy is weak and unemployment is high (e.g., 2009 and 2010). The demand for H-1B visas is therefore self-regulating, which is a very good argument for getting rid of the quota altogether.

Another argument for getting rid of the H-1B quota is that it makes planning very difficult for employers and H-1B employees alike. As you can see, in a good economy it is important to **file early**, before the quota is exhausted.

---

[2] In that year, April 1 fell on a Sunday, so April 2 was the first day petitions were accepted.

⇨ **Tip** Filing early generally means identifying the new H-1B employee early in the calendar year, obtaining an employment agreement in February, preparing the H-1B petition in March, and filing on April 1.

  Quota Exemptions

Only new H-1B petitions are counted against the quota. There are seven *exemptions* from the quota, including those who:

- Are already in H-1B status

- Were previously in H-1B status and had not reached the six-year limit

- Were never in H-1B status, but had an H-1B petition approved on their behalf

- Will be employed by a college or university

- Will be employed by an employer affiliated with a college or university

- Will be employed by a private-sector nonprofit research organization

- Will be employed by a government research organization

The most important of these exemptions is the exemption for those who are already in H-1B status. This exemption means that **employers can hire professionals already in H-1B status at any time of the year**.

Similarly, those who were **previously in H-1B status** may be exempt from the quota. For example, a husband and wife might both obtain H-1B visas to work in the United States. If one spouse—let's say the wife—later decides to stop working, she can change her status to H-4 (the nonworking status for dependents). If she later decides to change back to H-1B status, she will not be subject to the quota, because she was already counted in a prior year.

Even if an employee has never worked for a given H-1B employer, he is exempt from the quota if an H-1B petition was approved on his behalf. Let's assume, for example, that an employer, Antelope Corporation, files an H-1B petition for an employee on April 1 while the quota is still open. It is approved on May 1. On June 1, the quota is filled. On June 15, Antelope Corporation tells the employee that it does not wish to hire him after all, and it withdraws the H-1B petition. The employee then gets a job offer from Zebra Corporation, which agrees to submit an H-1B petition. Zebra Corporation can do this even though the quota has been filled, because the employee was previously counted against the quota when the Antelope Corporation petition was approved (even though he never worked for Antelope Corporation).

Other exemptions from the H-1B quota depend on the type of employer that is hiring the H-1B employee. Most importantly, H-1B employees who will work for a college or university are exempt from the quota. Most, but not all, US colleges and universities are considered *institutions of higher education* that are exempt from the quota. Generally, a qualified institution must meet all of the following criteria: [3]

- It admits only students with secondary school degrees or the equivalent

- It is authorized by a state to provide postsecondary education

- It offers the following:

  - A bachelor's degree OR

  - A two-year program that can be credited toward a bachelor's degree OR

  - A degree that is acceptable for admission into graduate or professional school OR

  - At least a one-year program of training that prepares students for employment in a recognized occupation

- It is a public or other nonprofit institution

- It is accredited

🗐 **Resource**   A list of accredited colleges and universities can be found on the website of the US Department of Education, at http://ope.ed.gov/accreditation/GetDownloadFile.aspx.

Another important exemption is for employers that are *affiliated* with a college or university. For example, many school districts have affiliation with universities for training student teachers, and nonprofit and government hospitals (including the Veterans Administration) may have affiliations with universities for training physicians.

---

[3] 20 USC § 1001.

USCIS has provided three tests for determining whether an employer is affiliated with a college or university, as follows:

- The employer has shared ownership or control through the same board of directors
- The employer is operated by a college or university
- The employer is "attached to" the college or university as a branch, member, or subsidiary

---

⇨ **Clarification**   What is the extent of the affiliation that is required to provide the exemption from the *training fee* (explained in Chapter 6)? USCIS attempted to answer this question in a 2006 memo.[4] It points out that the employer is exempt from the H-1B quota even if it is not one of the qualifying organizations, as long as the employee works "at" the qualifying organization and helps to further its objectives. Under this definition, an IT consulting company that has contracted with a college to develop its information systems would be exempt from the training fee if the H-1B employee will work at the college.

Another important exemption is for **nonprofit or government research institutions.** For this exemption to apply, the employer must be "primarily engaged in basic research and/or applied research." *Basic research* is defined in the H-1B regulations as "research to gain . . . knowledge . . . without specific applications in mind." *Applied research* includes "investigations oriented to discovering new scientific knowledge that has specific commercial objectives with respect to products, processes, or services."

An H-1B employee who is hired by one of these exempt organizations cannot transfer to a private company or other non-exempt employer without being counted against the quota. Such a transfer normally requires careful planning to avoid a gap in H-1B status. For example, a computer science professor working in H-1B status for a university (a quota-exempt employer) might get an employment offer from a software company (a non-exempt employer). If the quota for the year is filled (as it normally is), the company must file the H-1B petition on April 1 and wait for the employment to start October 1. However, an employee of a quota-exempt employer may transfer to another quota-exempt employer (for example, from a university to a nonprofit research institution) without waiting for the quota.

---

[4] www.uscis.gov/USCIS/Laws/Memoranda/Static_Files_Memoranda/Static_Files_Memoranda/Archives%201998-2008/2006/ac21c060606.pdf

Chapter Takeaway A general guideline for employers is that those already in H-1B status or who will work for an exempt organization may be hired at any time and may be added to the payroll almost immediately. Those new to H-1B status should be hired early in the year, but they cannot begin their employment until October 1.

Eligibility for H-1B Status

The H-1B application process should begin with an analysis of H-1B eligibility to determine the chances of success, the resources that will be needed in preparing the case, and whether it is worth it to proceed at all.

General Requirements of H-1B Petitions

There are two basic requirements for H-1B eligibility:

- The worker must have a bachelor's degree in a specialty field, *or equivalent training and experience*, and

- The job must normally require that degree.

One without the other is not sufficient. For example, a person with a bachelor's degree in accounting and a CPA designation is a professional accountant. However, if his proposed employment is to manage a retail store, that employment would not be eligible for H-1B classification, even though he would be using his accounting skills on a daily basis. That is because the position of store manager does not *normally* require a person with a degree in a specialty field like accounting.

Similarly, a highly skilled software engineer who worked as a software developer for five years but who never went to college would not be eligible for H-1B status. That is true even if she were offered a job that normally requires a bachelor's degree in computer science, and even if she could demonstrate that her expertise was the same as that of someone who had the specialty college degree. She may have written a book on the subject, completed complicated software development projects, and presented papers at international conferences. Nonetheless, if she does not have a bachelor's degree "or equivalent," she is not eligible.

Employee Requirements

The H-1B employee must be a **professional**. That is defined as someone who has either:

1. A US bachelor's degree in the specialty field in which he or she will work as an H-1B employee; or

2. A foreign degree that is equivalent to a US bachelor's degree in the specialty field; or

3. A combination of education, experience, and training that is *equivalent* to a US bachelor's degree in the specialty field.

Credentials Evaluations

Often it is not clear whether a bachelor's degree earned in another country is equivalent to a US bachelor's degree. If there is any doubt as to the equivalency, you can order a credential evaluation of foreign degrees and courses from a commercial evaluator.

Note Specific to India   In India, many bachelor's degrees are awarded after three years of college-level study, rather than the four years typically required in the US. Examples of three-year Indian degrees are Bachelor of Commerce, Bachelor of Computer Application, Bachelor of Arts, and Bachelor of Science. These degrees are *not* accepted by USCIS as equivalent to a US bachelor's degree, so additional experience, education, or training is required to be eligible for H-1B status. However, Bachelor of Engineering and Bachelor of Technology degrees in India are conferred after four years of college and will support an H-1B petition without any additional experience, education, or training.

By obtaining the credential evaluation before starting the H-1B case, you can determine whether additional documentation will be required to prove eligibility. We suggest using a credential evaluator that uses "EDGE," the same online credential evaluation service used by US Citizenship and Immigration Services (USCIS). There are dozens of foreign credential evaluators doing business in the US; their contact details and comparative services and fees are tabulated on the international admissions websites of many US colleges.[1]

The Three-for-One Rule

What is *equivalent* to a bachelor's degree? That is precisely defined in the H-1B regulations and usually involves the *three-for-one rule*. This rule provides that **three years of experience or training in the specialty field** will substitute for **each year of college the H-1B employee lacks.** For example, a person who attended two years of college and has six years of experience in the field would probably qualify for H-1B status because her combined education and experience would be considered equivalent to a bachelor's degree.

However, in our earlier example, the very knowledgeable and experienced software engineer who had not attended any college would not be eligible for H-1B status based on the three-for-one rule, because she had only 5 years of experience. Without any college education, she would need 12 years of experience to achieve equivalence to a bachelor's degree.

In order for experience and training to be considered equivalent to college study, they must be in "progressively responsible positions directly related to the specialty." Employment is normally *progressive*, since it is natural for an employee to be promoted over time, or to change jobs to more responsible positions. A person who remains in an entry-level job might not be able to establish the equivalent of a college degree based on experience and training.

⇨ **Tip**   An employee who does not have a college degree should start the process of getting letters from present and former employers proving prior experience as soon as possible. Those letters should state the job title, the dates the employment began and ended, and a description of each position held, including all of the tools and technologies used.

The best way to get such experience letters is to prepare them yourself, and then to give them to the employer as a Word document for final editing, printing onto company stationery, and signing. If you just ask the employer to write you a letter from scratch, it will be a low-priority item and you may never get it. It is also advisable to show the draft letter to your immigration attorney *before* giving it to the employer, so you do not have to ask the employer later for a revised letter. The attorney can evaluate not only whether the letter is acceptable for the H-1B case, but also whether it will be useful for a later green card (permanent residence) case.

---

[1] Such as www.dcccd.edu/Emp/Departments/EA/TS/forStudents/Pages/ForCredEvals.aspx.

The regulations require that those who seek to use the three-for-one rule must—in addition to proving three years of experience for each missing year of education—also meet **one** of the five following requirements:

- Demonstrate *"recognition of expertise in the specialty occupation by at least two recognized authorities in the same specialty occupation."* Often this is accomplished with a letter from a university professor in the field. There are also several for-profit businesses that prepare evaluations of experience. (Such "experience evaluations" should be distinguished from the "credential evaluations" discussed above.)

⇨ 🖋 **Tip** In practice, USCIS will often approve an H-1B petition with only one experience evaluation, rather than the two indicated in the regulation.

- Demonstrate membership in a recognized association or society in the specialty occupation.
- Submit published writings by or about the H-1B employee.
- Prove that the H-1B employee has been licensed in the profession.
- Demonstrate an achievement in the field that an expert deems to be "significant."

Most cases involving the three-for-one rule will rely on the first option: an experience evaluation by an expert (such as a professor). Generally, though, USCIS will not accept the conclusion of the evaluator, but will make its own determination as to whether the experience is equivalent to a specialty college degree. That determination is normally fairly straightforward, and if you submit good letters documenting the experience in the field, USCIS will usually find equivalency to a college degree.

It may therefore be more efficient in most cases that rely on the three-for-one rule to use the cheaper experience evaluations from the companies that provide them, rather than track down and retain a professor or other expert in the field to perform the evaluation. If USCIS is not satisfied with the experience evaluation, it will issue a **Request for Evidence** (**RFE**) and give the employer another chance to submit an experience evaluation or other additional evidence.

⇨ **Note** The risk that USCIS will issue a Request for Evidence can be minimized by submitting a well-documented and error-free petition, but some USCIS examiners will issue RFEs even in well-documented and clearly approvable cases. The RFE will delay the case and may cause some panic, but it is not the end of the world, and it does allow another opportunity to present evidence that is likely to result in an approval.

The decision as to what evidence to submit with the H-1B petition will vary according to the case, and cost, time, and efficiency should all be considered. Most H-1B employees have four-year college degrees, so cases involving the three-for-one rule are a small percentage of the H-1B cases that are filed.

License in Lieu of a College Degree

There is one other way of demonstrating eligibility for H-1B status besides a college degree or an equivalent of a college degree using the three-for-one rule. That is for the H-1B employee to hold a state license or certification that authorizes him or her to practice the profession. It is very unusual for a person to get H-1B status in this manner, because usually a state license requires a degree or experience that would make a person eligible for H-1B status without the license. However, it is conceivable that a person could qualify for H-1B status based on a license alone. For example, in California, a person without a college degree can obtain a license to practice law if he or she works with and is trained by an attorney for five years and then passes the bar examination. That person would not have the education or experience necessary for H-1B status, but could get H-1B status based on the license to practice law.

College Degree, but the Wrong One

Often a professional will have a college degree, but in a different field than the one in which she works. For example, a person may have a bachelor's degree in Business but work as a software developer. In this case, the three-for-one rule can be applied in much the same way it is when a person does not have any bachelor's degree at all. The first step is to determine, perhaps with the help of a credentials evaluator, how much of the college study can be counted toward the correct specialty degree.

A starting point is to recognize that the first year, or perhaps the first two years, of normal undergraduate study may involve courses outside of the major. That is especially true in a liberal arts college, where the student may take general courses in humanities, social sciences, and science before concentrating on the major field of study.

In our example involving the software developer with a major in Business, you would first decide on the appropriate degree in the specialty field to which you wish to demonstrate equivalency. Perhaps in this case it would be Information Systems. You could then find the curriculum of a US college that leads to that degree, perhaps on the college website. The courses required for the degree in Information Systems would be listed, and you could determine how many of the courses the employee took could be considered general courses (i.e., not specialty courses in the major) that would count toward the degree.

Let's assume you can demonstrate to USCIS that two years of the software developer's Business degree were general courses that would count toward the Information Systems major at a liberal arts college in the US. Assume further that the software developer also took courses that would count as courses within the Information Systems major. For example, she may have taken courses in Introductory Programming, Web Design, Management Information Systems, and Introduction to Mobile Applications—and those courses may equal an entire semester. That semester, added to the two years of general courses, would result in 2.5 years of courses that could count toward the major, leaving 1.5 years of education to be added using the three-for-one rule. With 4.5 years of experience (1.5 X 3), the person with the Business degree could establish that she has the equivalent of a degree in Information Systems.

The final consideration is whether the degree really is the wrong one. A degree in Business may be a specialty degree that qualifies a person for software development, especially if it is a Business degree with an MIS concentration. You need to analyze all of the courses taken and other experience and training to make a compelling case to USCIS that the employee has the equivalent of a bachelor's degree that is appropriate to the specialty field in which she will be working.

For example, we often see cases of people with bachelor's degrees in Electrical Engineering who seek H-1B status for applications software development positions. Normally, we would expect the appropriate degree to be in Computer Science or a similar field such as Information Technology. However, we can get this type of H-1B petition approved by documenting that the coursework in the Electrical Engineering curriculum can provide the required expertise in software development. In such a case we would obtain the course descriptions in the Electrical Engineering program, and if possible, the syllabus for each of those courses (indicating texts to be read, projects required, and technologies to be used). We would then hire a credential evaluator to review each of the courses and to identify those courses requiring high-level programming that would qualify a person for a career in applications software development.

Job Requirements

That brings us to the other major requirement for H-1B eligibility: not only must the H-1B employee have a specialty degree or equivalent, but the proposed H-1B employment must also require a specialty degree. The job must be in a *specialty occupation*—one that requires highly specialized knowledge that is normally attained through study leading to a bachelor's degree in that field.

Our analysis of the job then is really the flip side of our analysis of the employee's degree. We must demonstrate that one or more *specialty degrees* are an appropriate preparation for the job—in fact a normal minimum requirement for the job—and that the employee has one of those degrees or its equivalent.

What Is a "Specialty Degree"?

The case of *Residential Finance Corporation vs. USCIS* is instructive. The plaintiff, Residential Finance, petitioned for H-1B status for a market research analyst. USCIS denied the petition on the basis that the market research analyst position did not require a specialty degree. Residential Finance Corporation sought review of this decision by a federal court. The court scolded USCIS for its sloppy work and sloppy analysis, and overturned the denial. Specifically, it found that it was unreasonable to expect that a specialty job exactly match a specialty college major:

> There is no apparent requirement that the specialized study needed be in a single academic discipline as opposed to a specialized course of study in related business specialties. Defendant's [USCIS's] implicit premise that the title of a field of study controls ignores the realities of the statutory language involved and the obvious intent behind them. The knowledge and not the title of the degree is what is important. Diplomas rarely come bearing occupation-specific majors. What is required is an occupation that requires highly specialized knowledge and a prospective employee who has attained the credentialing indicating possession of that knowledge.

However, you do not want to have your H-1B petition denied and then win in court a few years later. You want to have your H-1B petition approved within a few weeks of filing it. To do that, you will need to make a compelling case that the job offered is a *specialty occupation*—a professional position that requires a specialty degree.

♟ ♟ Specialty Occupation

You have several tools you can use to convince the USCIS examiner that the job normally requires a specialty degree. For example, USCIS relies heavily on a publication of the US Department of Labor (DOL) called the *Occupational Outlook Handbook* (**OOH**). The *OOH*, which can be found at www.bls.gov/ooh/, describes various professions and discusses the normal qualifications for each. The *OOH* can help your case by establishing that:

- A specialty bachelor's degree is required for the profession
- The applicant's particular degree is relevant

For example, the *OOH* entry for *Software Developers* (reproduced in Appendix 4-2), states that they "usually have a bachelor's degree, typically in computer science, software engineering, or a related field" and that "a degree in mathematics is also acceptable." This entry is helpful to establish that the position normally requires a specialty college degree. In addition, if you have a degree in Mathematics, this *OOH* entry would establish that your educational background alone (i.e., without additional experience) makes you eligible for H-1B status.

However, the entry for *Computer Support Specialist* (Appendix 4-1) is not very helpful, and it may lead USCIS to believe that the proposed employment, for example for a Technical Support Engineer, is not a professional position. That is because the *OOH* states that "a bachelor's degree is required for some computer support specialist positions, but an associate's degree or postsecondary classes may be enough for others." The USCIS examiner could use this language as an excuse to deny the H-1B petition. Armed with knowledge of the *OOH* description, you would provide additional evidence in the petition to prove that the job offered is one of the "more technical" Computer Support Specialist positions that require a specialty bachelor's degree "in computer science, engineering, or information science."

Another publication of the DOL that analyzes the normal educational requirements for a job is O*NET (www.onetonline.org/). O*NET may be more or less helpful than the *OOH* in establishing that a degree is normally required for the profession. For example, for the Computer Support Specialist profession it is decidedly less helpful. Whereas the *OOH* indicates that a bachelor's degree is required for some Computer Support Specialist positions, the O*NET entry for that job states that "most occupations in this zone require training in vocational schools, related on-the-job experience, or an associate's degree."[2] USCIS rarely relies on O*NET alone to make its determination, but if it did, it probably would deny the H-1B petition for the Technical Support Engineer position. At the least, the *OOH* and O*NET would warn you that you cannot assume that an H-1B petition for a job in this occupational category will be approved unless it can be shown that a specialty degree or equivalent is necessary.

If the *OOH* and O*NET do not provide sufficient evidence of eligibility, you must submit additional evidence that the job requires a specialty college degree (and therefore is a "specialty occupation"). H-1B regulations provide four different tests for determining whether a job is a specialty occupation:[3]

- A bachelor's or higher degree or its equivalent is normally the minimum requirement for entry into the particular position;

- The degree requirement is common to the industry in parallel positions among similar organizations;

- The employer normally requires a degree or its equivalent for the position; and/or

- The job duties are so specialized and complex that knowledge required to perform them is usually associated with the attainment of a baccalaureate or higher degree.

⇨ **Tip** Although the regulations indicate that eligibility can be based on any one of these four criteria, in practice it is a good idea to establish eligibility under as many criteria as you can.

For example, in the case of the Technical Support Engineer, we cannot, based on the *OOH* or O*NET, establish that a bachelor's degree is a normal minimum requirement. Also, simply showing that you normally hire people with a bachelor's degree would not lead to an approval (despite the plain language of the regulation). You would therefore need to describe the position in detail and describe the complex technologies and computer science concepts that must be used in the job. You would need to distinguish the job—which may involve advanced technical support for other engineers, escalated support issues, bug fixes, complex computing and networking environments, and active liaison with software developers—from the majority of computer support jobs that do not require a degree (such as simple help-desk jobs that provide telephone support to consumer users).

---

[2] www.onetonline.org/link/summary/15-1151.00
[3] 8 CFR 214.2(h)(4)(iii)(A).

You could also get letters from other companies that hire highly skilled technical support engineers. Those letters could confirm that those companies require their own employees in similar positions to have specialty bachelor's degrees (or equivalent education and experience) and that the degree is a normal requirement in the industry for that type of computer technical support. Another way to prove your case would be to find classified employment ads indicating that bachelor's degrees are required for open technical support positions.

🏃 👤 Interplay between the Employee's Professional Background and the Determination of Whether the Job Is a Profession

Assessing the strength of your H-1B case before filing it with USCIS has two advantages. First, you can determine the amount of evidence you will need to submit with the petition, as well as the arguments you will need to make to convince USCIS that your case should be approved. If you have a borderline case, you will need to obtain extensive documentation of your professional background and the complexity of the job. Second, if you conclude that you have a weak case, you may decide that it is not worth all of the costs and effort required, because there is a good chance that the H-1B petition will be denied.

As with any human endeavor, there is a significant subjective component in the examiner's decision to approve or deny a borderline case. You should recognize that subjective element and assist the examiner in understanding that your case fulfills the letter *and spirit* of the H-1B laws by promoting their aim to import specialty skills that will benefit the science and commerce of the US. Although it is not mentioned in any of the H-1B statutes, regulations, or agency memos, there is an implicit understanding that H-1B employees are not ordinary workers who will take a non-specialty job away from an American. Certainly the USCIS examiner will have those sorts of concerns in mind when deciding on your application. It is important to take the time to describe the job duties in detail, making it clear that the job requires a high level of expertise that only highly educated workers can achieve.

We have found that the employee's background may affect the determination of whether the job normally requires a specialty bachelor's degree, and that the nature of the job can determine whether the employee is deemed a professional. A strong case that the employee is a professional may save an H-1B case in which it is not entirely clear that the job requires such a professional. Conversely, a weak professional background can be helped by a strong job offer. If both professional background and job are weak, the case is likely to be denied.

For example, in our case of the computer support specialist (where, as we have seen, some jobs require a specialty bachelor's degree and some do not), the background of the proposed employee may be a deciding factor. If the employee has a master's degree in computer science (i.e., an educational background that exceeds H-1B requirements), the USCIS examiner may conclude that the proposed job does indeed require a person with a high level of expertise.

On the other hand, if the employee does not have a college degree but qualifies as a computer support specialist under the three-for-one rule, the USCIS examiner will likely conclude that a college degree is not required.

Moreover, an employee may qualify for H-1B status only by using the three-for-one rule and have a weak case for demonstrating such eligibility, yet benefit from the fact that the offered job is one for which a college degree is almost always required. For example, a person without a college degree may have worked for many years as a laboratory technician—a nonprofessional position. However, if she is offered a job as laboratory supervisor, and the employer can demonstrate that the laboratory supervisor normally has an advanced degree (master's or PhD), USCIS may agree that the experience as a laboratory technician prepared the employee to accept that high-level professional position.

♞ ♝ Salary

Salary is another key element in determining H-1B eligibility. In Chapter 8, we will discuss the **Required Wage**—the salary the employer must pay to make sure that H-1B employment does not depress the salaries of American professionals. However, USCIS will also look at the salary as part of its determination that the job really is a professional position that requires a bachelor's degree or equivalent.

Returning to the example of the Computer Support Specialist (an occupation for which some jobs require a degree and some do not), salary is likely to have a major impact on whether the petition will be approved. A salary of $50,000 per year would probably exceed the Prevailing Wage required by the DOL for a Computer Support Specialist. However, that salary probably would lead USCIS to conclude that the job does not require a person with a specialty degree. On the other hand, a salary of $100,000 would be a simple and eloquent way to communicate the idea that the job involves exceptional complexity and requires a professional computer engineer.

Examples of Difficult H-1B Eligibility Cases

To illustrate typical strategies for demonstrating H-1B eligibility in questionable cases, we have culled a few examples from the thousands of successful H-1B cases we have handled.[4] These cases are not intended to provide templates for handling your own case but to illustrate some of the concepts discussed above.

Hotel Manager with a Literature Degree

The owners of a resort hotel asked us to obtain an H-1B visa for a woman they had hired to be the general manager. She had a bachelor's degree in literature, but her parents had owned a restaurant, and she had worked in the hospitality industry (restaurants and hotels) for twenty years.

We had two problems with this case. First, it was questionable whether she had the equivalent of a specialty college degree in hotel management; second, it was questionable whether the job required such a degree. Therefore, the application was weak in terms of the two prongs of eligibility (professional background and job). As discussed above, such cases are usually denied.

We started with the requirements in the *OOH*:

> *Many applicants may qualify with a high school diploma and long-term experience working in a hotel. However, most large, full-service hotels require applicants to have a bachelor's degree. Hotels that provide fewer services generally accept applicants who have an associate's degree or certificate in hotel management or operations.*

As you can see, the *OOH* focuses on the size of the hotel and the services it provides. We therefore had to demonstrate the nature of the hotel, which also had an attached restaurant, and its operations. We gathered marketing brochures, a copy of the hotel's website, its tax return, payroll records, and other documents that reflected the number of beds, number of guests, number of employees, and revenue. We listed each of the employees by job title and described their functions. We also listed all of the vendors who provided services to the hotel (since the hotel manager would also supervise purchases from those vendors). We provided an organizational chart that depicted the hotel manager's managerial role. Finally, we submitted

---

[4] Minor details of these cases have been changed to protect client confidentiality.

architectural plans and other documents that showed planned expansion and renovation, and we explained in our supporting letter that the hotel manager would also be responsible for construction planning as an advisor to the board of directors.

We then described each of the proposed job duties of the hotel manager and assigned a percentage of time the H-1B employee would spend on each. Those duties included such broad categories as day-to-day operations and planning (for example, budget responsibility and planning to maximize profits), accounting (overseeing the accounting staff), business development and marketing, and food and beverage supervision.

Fortunately, the H-1B employee was still in contact with her previous employers in the hospitality industry, and we were able to work with those employers to assemble detailed letters describing the size of their restaurant and resort operations and outlining the employee's responsibilities. Altogether, we were able to demonstrate sufficient experience to show progressive responsibility for at least 12 years.

Our final task was to compare her background with the expertise gained in a course of study leading to a bachelor's degree in hotel administration. We chose Cornell University, the premier college in the US for this type of study, and submitted to USCIS a copy of Cornell's web pages describing its bachelor's, master's, and PhD programs in hotel administration. We also submitted a list of the courses required for the bachelor's degree, along with a description of the courses (also on the Cornell website). Those courses included such things as Hospitality Facilities Management, Hospitality Development and Planning, Accounting, Food Service Operations, and Hotel Operations. We then explained how our client gained the expertise conferred by those courses through her past experience, by relating each course to the detailed job descriptions included in her experience letters. Finally, we explained how the expertise gained in each of the college courses was necessary for the proposed H-1B employment. Based on this extensive documentation, the USCIS approved the H-1B petition.

IT Worker with a PhD in a Non-Computer Field

An individual was hired as a computer systems analyst to perform an analysis of business requirements (such as HR functions) and to develop information systems for the employer's clients. The job duties mostly involved implementing Oracle applications in a variety of computing environments and developing custom applications software to fill in company-specific gaps not covered by the standard Oracle software. An important part of the job was to use tools such as data mining and computer modeling to map business processes.

The employee had a PhD degree in physics, but he had never taken computer science courses (other than introductory programming courses) and had no prior paid experience as an IT worker.

It was clear that the job duties would normally require a person with a degree in Information Systems or Computer Science. The *OOH* states that "most computer systems analysts have a bachelor's degree in a computer-related field."[5] Physics is not explicitly a "computer-related field." However, in this case, we could demonstrate the H-1B employee's extensive use of computer modeling in his research projects in physics, as well as the use of data visualization tools to convert three-dimensional data into graphs and movies. The employee's professor, with the assistance of the employee, wrote a detailed letter describing the various computer programs and software tools he had used in connection with class projects and his PhD thesis.

This petition was successful. Even though the employee did not have a specialty degree in the field of software development, we established that he had the specialty skills required for the job. Perhaps USCIS heeded the admonition in *Residential Finance Corporation v. USCIS* that "diplomas rarely come bearing occupation-specific majors" and that the prospective employee need only demonstrate that he "has attained the credentialing indicating possession of that knowledge."

Plant Manager with No College Education

A small US manufacturer wanted to hire a Plant Manager from Germany, because he had experience with the machinery the company had recently purchased. The duties of the Plant Manager were to act as shop foreman and to supervise production employees in the operation, repair, and maintenance of the machinery. He was to establish and supervise maintenance schedules, establish redundant systems and machinery, and make sure that revenues would not be lost because of production machinery downtime.

In this case, the employee did not have a college education, but he had worked in factories for 25 years, working his way up through the ranks from apprentice to machine operator to shop foreman. He was an expert in the repair, maintenance, and operation of various types of complex machinery, as well as manufacturing systems and processes. We were able to get letters from former employers documenting this experience in detail. In addition, he had attended several vocational courses and had certificates to confirm his completion of those courses.

---

[5] www.bls.gov/ooh/computer-and-information-technology/computer-systems-analysts. htm#tab-4.

We then established that the proposed job duties of the Plant Manager were those of a Mechanical Engineer, using the O*NET description.[6] We listed each of the duties that were common to the Mechanical Engineer occupation and the Plant Manager position, including:

- Develop, coordinate, and monitor all aspects of production, including selection of manufacturing methods, fabrication, and operation of product designs.

- Read and interpret blueprints, technical drawings, schematics, and computer-generated reports.

- Research, design, evaluate, install, operate, and maintain mechanical products, equipment, systems and processes to meet requirements, applying knowledge of engineering principles.

- Confer with engineers and other personnel to implement operating procedures, resolve system malfunctions, and provide technical information.

- Recommend design modifications to eliminate machine or system malfunctions.

- Investigate equipment failures and difficulties to diagnose faulty operation, and to make recommendations to maintenance crew.

- Specify system components or direct modification of products to ensure conformance with engineering design and performance specifications.

However, establishing that the job duties were those of a Mechanical Engineer was not the end of the inquiry, because O*NET also states that "most of these occupations require a four-year bachelor's degree, but some do not." We had to demonstrate that the job was like *most* of the jobs in the occupational category, i.e., those that require the four-year degree.

Fortunately, the General Manager of the factory had a degree in Manufacturing Engineering, and we could show that up to that point he had undertaken the role of Plant Manager. Also, we were able to get letters from other small manufacturers confirming that their production managers had similar college degrees.

---

[6] www.onetonline.org/link/summary/17-2141.00

Finally, we pointed out in our supporting letter that the proposed employee had rare knowledge of the machinery the company had purchased. The letter explained that his knowledge was crucial to the success of implementing the machinery, and that the machinery represented a major investment by the employer. We reminded USCIS that small manufacturers in the US faced intense competition from overseas, and that the company's success, and its ability to continue employing over twenty production workers, could be affected if it were not able to hire the Plant Manager. Although not directly relevant to the specific matters in the H-1B regulations (i.e., whether the employee was a professional and whether the job was a professional job), this argument was relevant to the larger issue of the purpose of the H-1B visa: to bring the skills of talented and highly educated people to the US in support of the US economy.

It is important to remember that USCIS examiners are people too, and that they would naturally like to see American business and manufacturing succeed. If you can make a compelling case that the H-1B employee will be essential to a company's success and that the H-1B employee will not take a job away from an American, you may save a borderline case. That is true even though neither corporate success nor protection of US workers is mentioned in any of the statutes, regulations, and agency guidance that define H-1B eligibility!

Conclusion

An analysis of H-1B eligibility should begin the H-1B process, to determine the chances of success, the resources that will be needed in preparing the case, and whether it is worth it to proceed at all. Also, attention should be paid to properly documenting eligibility, with respect to both the employee's professional background and the nature of the job. Even jobs that you believe are obviously professional positions should be described in detail, and you will need to explain why a specialty college degree is required.

In 2012, USCIS began to question whether many IT jobs really require a specialty degree, issuing increasing numbers of RFEs and denials based on this issue. The problem became so severe that the American Immigration Lawyers Association (AILA) collected evidence of the RFEs and denials in order to complain to USCIS of this policy shift. It is all the more advisable, when USCIS is applying requirements more restrictively and issuing RFEs and denials more freely, that the H-1B employer and employee work up a thorough analysis of the professional nature of the proposed employment and present USCIS with a persuasive case that the job requires a specialty college degree or equivalent.

Complementary Roles of the H-1B Employee, Sponsor, and Attorney

The prospective H-1B employee and her sponsoring employer have complementary roles in the H-1B process, and it behooves both parties to cooperate knowledgeably and harmoniously to effect their shared goal of enabling the candidate to accept the proposed employment. The attorney is primarily the liaison and facilitator in the employer's interactions with US Citizenship and Immigration Services. But because of the closely coupled interests of the employee and employer in this project, the attorney generally represents the employee as well as the employer, within stipulated limits. The interlocking roles of these three actors are described in turn in this chapter.

The Role of the Prospective H-1B Employee

The H-1B employee probably has the most at stake in the H-1B process. Whereas the employer is merely gaining a skilled employee, the prospective H-1B visa holder has made the life-changing decision to live and work in America, at least for several years.

With the most to gain and the most to lose, the employee therefore should be actively involved in the H-1B case and should ask to be kept informed of all developments in the case.

Most importantly, the prospective employee must gather the documents and provide the information that is essential to success in the case and should do so as quickly as possible. For those already in H-1B status, that should be a fairly simple task—probably just a matter of providing documents used in the previous H-1B petition. For those seeking H-1B status for the first time, some thought and care should be invested in selecting and providing the necessary documents (described in Chapter 7).

In addition to providing information and documents necessary for preparation of the petition, the employee must:

1. Apply for the H-1B visa at a US consulate or embassy (see Chapters 2 and 7);

2. Present sufficient documentation to gain entry into the US at an international airport or US land border (see Chapter 7); and

3. Calendar and track H-1B status, as well as H-4 status for family members, on forms I-94 (see Chapter 10).

The Role of the Hiring Manager

Upon identifying a prospective employee who may need an H-1B visa, and before extending any offers, the hiring manager should give the job description and the employee's résumé to the human resources (HR) department for forwarding to the immigration attorney. There are two reasons for this important first step. First, the immigration attorney can evaluate and provide feedback as to whether there are any obstacles to obtaining the H-1B status. Those obstacles might include the employee's background, the nature of the offered job, or the H-1B quota. Second, the immigration attorney can evaluate and provide feedback on the Required Wage (see Chapter 8). It is a waste of everyone's time to extend a job offer only to later find out that the offered salary is too low to support an H-1B petition, that the job or employee is ineligible for H-1B status, or that an H-1B visa will not be immediately available because of the H-1B quota.

Before extending any job offers, the hiring manager must also get a good idea of how long it will take to obtain the H-1B visa. That information is crucial because it may not be practical to hire an individual if the employment cannot start soon. By providing all information to the attorney at a very early stage, the hiring manager should be able to get a fairly good estimate as to when the employment can begin.

⇨ **Note**   Generally, the expected start date will depend on whether the employee is already in H-1B status working for another employer. Employees in that situation may be able to move to their new employers within a week or so, because they are able to begin their employment as soon as the H-1B petition is filed (i.e., they do not have to wait until it is approved). However, potential employees who are outside of the United States, or who are in another visa status, must wait for the petition to be approved (and if outside the United States must also wait for a visa) before beginning the employment. Also, in some cases the employee must wait several months, and potentially up to a year, for visas to become available under the H-1B quota (see Chapter 3).

Often the H-1B employee will have multiple job offers, in either the United States or the home country, so it is important to reassure the employee that the company will obtain the H-1B petition expeditiously.

The most important role of the hiring manager is to provide a detailed job description, including the job title, suggested salary, and education and experience requirements. Not only will that determine H-1B eligibility, but it will also give the attorney the data needed to estimate the correct *Prevailing Wage.*

The hiring manager should also ascertain the salaries of the other employees already working for the company in a similar capacity. That will enable the employer to determine the *Actual Wage.* Generally, other employees who are doing similar work should not be paid more, unless there is a good reason for the difference. Those good reasons might include more years of experience in the field, more experience with company-specific technologies, or a higher academic degree (see Chapter 8).

The salary offered to the H-1B employee should be the higher of the Prevailing Wage and the Actual Wage—denominated the *Required Wage.* The Required Wage should be determined before an offer is extended to the employee, to avoid having to obtain internal company approval for the salary a second time or having to retract an offer because the salary is too low.

In negotiating with the potential H-1B employee, the hiring manager may also need to look ahead to permanent residence (green card) sponsorship. Normally the employer will have a set policy for sponsoring green cards—for example, one year after the employment begins. Such a policy assures the employee that the company will assist in securing his or her right to live permanently in the United States. At the same time, such a policy ensures that company resources are not spent until the H-1B employee has made a substantial commitment to the company, demonstrated loyalty, and proven to be a worker whom the company would like to retain long term.

It often makes sense to relax the normal policy for green card sponsorship. For example, the new employee may already have been in H-1B status for several years and may need to start a green card case right away to avoid running out of time under the H-1B time limit (see Chapter 10). Or the employee may have other job offers. Including the possibility of immediate green card sponsorship, which often is more valuable to immigrant employees than a higher salary, may give the prospective employer a competitive advantage in attracting the employee. The hiring manager should discuss these issues with HR and be prepared to negotiate and extend offers that include a discussion of later green card sponsorship.

The Role of the Employer's Human Resources Department

In addition to the normal tasks associated with hiring a new employee, the human resources director or manager has a special role in hiring new H-1B employees and must coordinate the H-1B petition process. To begin with, *before* any offer is made, there should be clear communication to make sure that the hiring manager takes the steps described above (i.e., providing HR with the candidate's résumé, detailed job description, and proposed salary). Too often, the hiring manager will present the job offer as a *fait accompli* and ask HR to obtain the necessary working visa. That can lead to difficult and embarrassing situations, especially when the hiring manager is also a top company executive or has already made significant plans to incorporate the new employee into the organization.

➪ **Note** This discussion assumes a large and compartmentalized organization. However, H-1B visas are not just for large corporations. At smaller companies, the hiring manager, HR director, and top executive might all be the same person!

HR should also assist the hiring manager in determining the Required Wage, since the job offer should not be made without that information. That will involve working with the attorney to determine the proper occupational category and the "level" to be used, based on several factors such as the minimum education and experience requirements, whether the H-1B employee will supervise other employees, and whether there are special requirements such as a particular license or language requirement. HR can also supply the Actual Wage by surveying all current employees who do similar work and who have similar backgrounds.

HR is normally the primary company contact with the immigration attorney and will be responsible for providing the attorney with the documents and information necessary to prepare the petition. Often, the HR director or HR manager will sign the H-1B petition, but it can be signed by anyone in the company who has the authority to sign. Job titles of those who sign H-1B petitions typically include President, Chief Financial Officer, Vice President, and Chief Technical Officer. In cases where one of these officers is signing, the HR person responsible for visa cases would review and then present the completed petition to that person. Since parts of the H-1B petition, particularly the Labor Condition Application (LCA), involve potential liability for the company, HR should carefully review all factual statements and make sure they are accurate before signing the H-1B petition or presenting it for signing.

H-1B cases also present a special circumstance in the generally required verification of documents proving the right to work on Form I-9, Employment Eligibility Verification. With very few exceptions, such as someone in H-1B status, authorized US workers are either US citizens or permanent residents. In those cases, HR collects and photocopies a document that proves identity, such as a driver's license, and a document that proves the right to work, such as a social security card. The employee checks a box on the I-9 confirming US citizenship or permanent resident (green card) status. For such employees, once the I-9 is completed at the time of hire, nothing more needs to be done. However, unlike US citizenship or permanent resident status, H-1B status is temporary, and the I-9 must reflect the expiration date. When the H-1B status is renewed, the I-9 must be updated. That requires a system to calendar the expiration date to make sure the I-9 is timely renewed.

⇨ **Tip**   You can complete an I-9 for an H-1B employee who is *porting* (i.e., transferring from one employer in H-1B status to another) as soon as the H-1B petition is filed. In our office, we use the FedEx delivery confirmation as evidence of filing. You can use the employee's passport, previous H-1B approval notice (for the other company), Form I-94, and evidence of filing your H-1B petition as proof of the right to work. In that case, you should write "AC21" in the margin of the I-9 (see page 17 of the I-9 Handbook[1]). Calendar the I-9 and remember to update it when you receive the H-1B approval notice (Form I-797), which may be several months from the time of filing.

---

[1] www.uscis.gov/files/form/m-274.pdf

It is important that HR track the H-1B expiration dates, not only for I-9 updating but also to timely apply for an H-1B extension. USCIS rules permit filing for an extension up to six months before expiration, and it is a good idea to file for extensions as early as possible. Petition processing times may be four or five months, and by filing early you can avoid the necessity of paying for expedited processing (*Premium Processing*) in the event that the employee needs to travel overseas or requires approval of the extension petition for some other reason (such as renewing a driver's license).

The Role of the Immigration Attorney

The attorney is the primary liaison between the sponsoring employer and USCIS. It is the attorney's job to collect the information and documents that establish eligibility for H-1B status, prepare the forms and other parts of the petition, and submit them to USCIS. In addition, the attorney will make legal arguments, conduct research, and request reconsideration or appeal to persuade USCIS that a particular H-1B petition should be approved.

In addition to this primary role of assembling and submitting a persuasive petition, the attorney has the following responsibilities:

- Advise the employer regarding potential problems with the H-1B petition and legal and ethical ways to fix those problems. Identify and correct weaknesses in the case.

- Provide information about LCA liability and explore strategies to comply with LCA obligations.

- Keep track of changes in the laws and policies of USCIS, as reflected in legislation, regulations, court decisions, administrative decisions, and policy memos.

- Consult with HR to devise effective strategies for hiring international employees based on the entire range of employment-based visas and green cards.

- Assist in drafting clear and persuasive supporting letters.

- Make sure that the H-1B petition and LCA meet all formal requirements, that deadlines are met, and that procedures are followed.

In fulfilling these responsibilities in an H-1B case, the attorney normally must represent both the employee and the employer. Both parties have an interest in having an attorney/client relationship.

The employer is the clearly the attorney's client, because it is the employer's petition and because it is the employer who typically pays the legal fee. The attorney provides advice and representation to the employer not only in connection with a particular H-1B petition, but also in connection with the employer's global immigration strategy (which may involve other H-1B cases, other types of nonimmigrant visas, permanent residence status, and such things as the effect of mergers and acquisitions on the immigration status and right to work of its international employees).

The employee too will normally have immigration questions and doubts that are beyond the expertise of the HR professional or the information in this book. Those questions may involve H-1B eligibility, eligibility for other types of visas, green card eligibility, US citizenship, and timing and procedures for obtaining the visa. Employees may have unique immigration issues that affect their ability to come to the US, such as prior denial of a visa, prior violation of H-1B or other nonimmigrant status, an arrest or criminal conviction, or other grounds for inadmissibility.

For example, an employee might previously have been in J-1 status[2] in the United States, which can trigger a requirement to return to her home country for two years. Or an employee might have made a misrepresentation in connection with a previous visa application. In that case, the attorney can help determine whether the misrepresentation makes him inadmissible and, if so, whether a waiver of inadmissibility can be obtained. Many H-1B professionals have questions about the ability of their spouses to work, study, or start businesses in the US, and whether another working visa or green card might be available to them. Most H-1B employees have questions about how to get US permanent residence status and how long it will take. The employee may also need advice and counsel regarding those aspects of the case for which the employee is responsible, primarily the application for the visa, and the application for admission into the United States. The attorney may need to contact the US embassy or consulate directly to resolve visa problems, and for that, the State Department requires a document (usually Form G-28) that confirms the attorney/client relationship with the employee. Attorneys can clarify and correct rumors and misinformation about H-1B eligibility and processing that abound on internet chat rooms.

Clearly, it would be inefficient and cumbersome to sift the employee's questions and other communications through HR or another employer representative, when they might be answered quickly and clearly by an email or telephone call to an attorney. But it usually is not cost-effective to hire two lawyers: one for the employer and one for the employee. Accordingly, one

---

[2] J-1 visas are used for training and internships in the United States (see Chapter 12).

immigration lawyer typically represents both employer and employee in H-1B cases. That can create the potential for conflicts of interest, particularly concerning issues of salary and termination of employment. For that reason, almost all states require lawyers to obtain prior consent in writing when they represent two different parties (with potentially conflicting interests) in the same case. In Appendix 5-1, we provide an example of the type of Dual Representation Consent we use in our office to inform the parties that there is an attorney/client relationship, define the limits of that relationship, warn about potential conflicts of interest, and confirm consent to this arrangement of our representing both parties.

The formation of the attorney/client relationship triggers many obligations that attorneys have to their clients. Those obligations include at a minimum 1) strict confidentiality, 2) diligence, 3) keeping you informed, 4) competence, and 5) avoiding conflicts of interest that might jeopardize those obligations. As a client in an immigration case, whether you are the employer or the employee, you should expect those obligations to be fulfilled, and you should engage a new attorney if they are not.

As reflected in the sample Dual Representation Consent, the attorney may limit and define the nature of these obligations, as long as those limitations are communicated in advance and as long as they are consistent with the rules that govern the attorney's professional conduct. For example, in our arrangement with our clients, we keep the employer's financial information confidential from the employee, and the employee's criminal or health problems confidential from the employer.

Conclusion

If all parties work together diligently, the H-1B petition process can be efficient and successful. In addition to the employee, employer, and attorney, there are other partners integral to the process, not emphasized in our discussion above. Those partners are the various government agencies that process, investigate, and grant H-1B status and visas: US Citizenship and Immigration Services, Department of Labor, Department of State, and Customs and Border Protection. As partners in the process, those agencies should not be fooled, lied to, or presented with sloppy work that makes their job more difficult. If you are in an antagonistic relationship with the government, you will lose! In subsequent chapters we will show you how to work together with the government agencies to present a winning case and avoid H-1B liability.

Employer Inputs to the H-1B Process

As described in Chapter 2, the H-1B process involves working with four different US government agencies: **DOL**,[1] **USCIS**,[2] **DOS**,[3] and **CBP**.[4] Generally, the employer is primarily responsible for interaction with the first two agencies, and the employee for interaction with the last two. This chapter will discuss the employer's inputs into the process necessary to successfully navigate the H-1B case through the DOL and USCIS, from the first steps to petition approval. Although these processes initially may seem daunting, the employer normally will be assisted by an immigration attorney. Often the time commitment by HR to H-1B cases can be limited to an hour or two per case.

Preparing the Job Description and Drafting Minimum Requirements

The first step in an H-1B case is to consider the job duties and the reasonable minimum requirements for the position. This job description is one of the most importance elements in the H-1B case, not only because it will be the

---

[1] Department of Labor.

[2] United States Citizenship and Immigration Services.

[3] Department of State (US embassies and consulates abroad).

[4] Customs and Border Protection.

basis for USCIS's determination of whether the job is a professional position that normally requires a specialty college degree, but also because it will be ingredient to its determination of the *Required Wage.*

In some cases, it may be tempting to embellish the job description to make it appear more like a specialty job (for example, to make a bookkeeper position seem more like an accountant position, or a consumer help-desk position seem more like a sophisticated technical support position). However, in such situations it is far better to avoid the H-1B case altogether than to lose credibility with USCIS or cross the line into fraud, with its attendant civil and criminal penalties. Clearly, false job descriptions should be avoided, but misleading job descriptions should be avoided as well, even if constructed to be factually accurate. The goal is to partner with USCIS to explain the job and the H-1B eligibility of the applicant, not to deceive them.

However, it is also important to give some thought to preparing the job description so it will be clear to USCIS that the job duties require expertise that is normally gained through specialized college study. It is helpful to list the various job duties together with the type of knowledge needed to perform them and the percentage of time to be spent on each. Indeed, USCIS often will ask for that sort of breakdown of time spent on each task, so it can be helpful to provide that information in advance. By going through this exercise, you can also get a better idea of whether you should file the H-1B petition at all. For example, a marketing job that involves both competitive market analysis using sophisticated computer modeling and making sales calls may be a good H-1B case if the market analysis part is 70 percent of the job. However, USCIS may conclude that it is not a professional position if 70 percent of the time is to be spent on sales calls.

Often the employer will have generic job descriptions used for internal hiring and organizational purposes, but those may not adequately describe the particular job the H-1B employee will be hired to do or the skills involved. It is a good idea for HR to contact the person who will ultimately manage the H-1B employee to identify exactly what the job duties will be and how much time will be spent on each task.

The employer should also be flexible in assigning a job title to the position, to the extent permitted by the company's internal organization and to the extent that it is accurate and not intended to deceive. Smaller employers generally have more flexibility in defining job titles, but large corporations should also consider modifying job titles in H-1B cases. For example, the job title of "Web Developer" may cause USCIS to doubt that the job is a professional position, because the DOL publications, discussed in Chapter 4, indicate that it is not. A high school or junior college web development course may be sufficient for many web developer positions. However, other web development positions, especially for consumer-facing websites that involve lots of data, may involve sophisticated software development, database, network, and server expertise, making a professional background essential. In those cases, it may be helpful to change the job title to something that better communicates the nature of the prospective employee's duties, such as "Software Developer" or "Applications Software Engineer."

The job description will be incorporated into the company letter that accompanies the H-1B petition, which is normally prepared by the immigration attorney. It should not be general but as specific as possible. It should explain the technologies, expertise, and education required to perform the various job duties.

If USCIS is not satisfied with the job description, and how that job description reflects the need for a person with a specialty bachelor's degree, it will return a **Request for Evidence** (RFE) asking for a fuller explanation. Typically lengthy, burdensome, and clad in irrelevant "boilerplate," an RFE can delay your case.

Careful attention should also be given to the minimum education, experience, and other requirements needed to do the job. These job requirements will impact the employee's immigration case in several ways:

- The job requirements will establish whether the job meets the threshold requirement for H-1B eligibility (i.e., whether it normally requires a bachelor's degree in a specialty field or equivalent).

- The job requirements will determine the *Required Wage* (discussed in Chapter 8). Generally, a requirement of more education and more experience means the employer will have to pay the employee a higher salary to meet the LCA requirements (discussed in this chapter).

- The job requirements may influence not only the H-1B case but also later eligibility for permanent residence status, if an H-1B employee is contemplating immigrating to the United States (i.e., applying for a green card) at some later date, A job that requires a master's degree, or a bachelor's degree plus five years of experience, is eligible for faster green card processing than jobs that require less education and/or experience. You may incur questions about your consistency and credibility if you claim that a job requires a bachelor's degree for the H-1B case, and then claim that a master's degree is required when it comes time to pursue the green card case.

As with the job description, it is important to be honest and try to accurately define the minimum requirements needed for a particular job. That definition may be based on past hiring practices, or on a realistic assessment of the skills, experience, and academic background required to do the particular job to be filled by the H-1B employee. Again, the generic company job description may not be an accurate statement of what is required for the job. For example, the existing job description may indicate that "a bachelor's or associate's degree" is the minimum academic requirement. However, a review of the company's hiring for that position might reveal that no one has ever been hired for it without a bachelor's degree. Or it might turn out that employees without a bachelor's degree were hired, but that they had extensive experience that was equivalent to a bachelor's degree (based on the "three-for-one rule" discussed in Chapter 4).

 # Company Information

The employer, assisted by the immigration attorney, will also need to present to USCIS sufficient evidence about the company. This information is typically summarized in the company letter that accompanies the H-1B petition, supplemented by various supporting documents.

There are several reasons why USCIS may need this information. First, it must determine whether the company really has the resources and the need to hire the H-1B employee. Second, the size of the company may determine the need for a professional employee. There are many professional positions in a large company that would not be appropriate in a smaller organization. For example, a full-time IT professional, accountant, or lawyer normally would not be needed in a company of less than ten employees (unless that company were in the business of IT consulting, accounting, or law). If the size of the company would not usually support the described position, USCIS may conclude that the employment—and the H-1B petition—is simply an accommodation for a friend or relative, or that the employer is using the H-1B process to attempt to hire a highly skilled professional for a nonprofessional position (such as office manager, bookkeeper, or legal secretary).

The quantity of information and documents that should be provided will vary according to the size of the company. Often, a copy of a few pages of the website of a large multinational company is sufficient to establish the company's existence, products, services, and need for the H-1B employee. If the stock is publicly traded, an annual report or SEC Form 10-K may be included with the petition.

Smaller companies have a greater burden in establishing their existence and size and the nature of their business. Suggested documents that might be included with the petition include the following:

- Website pages

- Lease for office premises

- Corporate tax return (e.g., Form 1120)

- Payroll records such as quarterly state returns and federal Forms 941. (Be careful not to reveal confidential information about other employees.)

- Business license

- Evidence of state corporation filings or registration

- Articles of incorporation

- Photographs of offices or other work locations (including, if possible, the desk or other location where the H-1B employee will work)

- Ads and marketing collateral

As with all of the documents submitted with the H-1B petition, original documents are rarely needed; photocopies are almost always sufficient. However, color photographs have the most impact and should be submitted where possible.

The Labor Condition Application

The Labor Condition Application (LCA) is such an essential part of the H-1B case that we are going to discuss it twice: here, as part of the employer's "to do list," and in more detail in Chapters 8 and 9, where we explore the LCA requirements and how to avoid penalties for noncompliance.

The LCA filing starts the clock on the H-1B processing time, so it is important to post the job notices and file the LCA at the earliest possible time. As of this writing, it typically takes the Department of Labor approximately one week to process the LCA. The rest of the petition—H-1B forms, supporting letter, supporting documents, and filing fees—can be prepared, signed, and assembled during the week that the LCA is pending, so that no time is lost. The first task in an H-1B case therefore should be filing the LCA, especially if you want the employee to start work soon.

Preparing and Filing the LCA

The LCA is filed electronically with the Department of Labor on **Form ETA-9035.**[5] That is done through the DOL's iCERT website at http://icert.doleta.gov. Normally the employer's attorney will create an account on iCERT to file and track LCAs, but the employer may do that directly instead.

The LCA contains the employer's name and address, the *Prevailing Wage* (more about that in Chapter 8), and the salary offered to the H-1B employee. However, it does not include the employee's name, which means that it can be used for multiple employees. Nevertheless, we recommend preparing a new LCA for each H-1B employee to avoid confusion in LCA administration and compliance.

In addition to this company-specific and job-specific information, the LCA contains the following promises the company must make:

- For the entire period of authorized employment, the employer will pay the H-1B employee the *Required Wage.*[6]

- The employment of the H-1B alien will not adversely affect the working conditions of workers similarly employed in the area of intended employment.

- On the date the LCA was signed and submitted, there was no strike, lockout, or work stoppage related to a labor dispute in the relevant occupation at the place of employment.

- Notice of the application was posted at the place of employment.

Posting of LCA Notices

Before the LCA can be filed, two identical legal notices must be posted at the place where the employee is to work. The LCA notices must be posted for 10 calendar days, but you do not have to wait the 10 days before filing the LCA. These two steps (LCA processing and posting) therefore may go on concurrently as long as the LCA notices are physically or electronically posted before the LCA is filed—even if only five minutes before. The content, posting locations, and manner of posting LCA notices is discussed in detail in Chapter 8.

---

[5] www.foreignlaborcert.doleta.gov/pdf/ETA_Form_9035.pdf

[6] The *Required Wage* is discussed in Chapter 8.

Preparing the Actual Wage Memorandum

The **Actual Wage Memorandum** is prepared by the employer to describe how the salary paid to the H-1B employee compares with that of other workers in the same company. It must state the wage to be paid to the H-1B employee and, according to the DOL's regulations, show "how the wage paid [to the H-1B employee] relates to all other [employees] with similar experience and qualifications for the specific employment in question." The Actual Wage Memorandum must be detailed enough to enable a third party to "understand how the employer applied its pay system to arrive at the actual wage for its H-1B nonimmigrant(s)."

The Actual Wage Memorandum must state the business-related factors that are used in setting wages and the manner in which they are implemented (for example, the salary range for the position and the pay differentials for various factors such as education, job experience, job duties, and demonstrated past performance). Finally, the Actual Wage Memorandum must explain that the benefits provided to the H-1B employee are consistent with the benefits provided to other employees.

Preparing the LCA File ("Public Access File")

The **public access file** is separate from the employee's personnel file. It must be made available to interested parties who request to see it. Those interested parties may include the H-1B employee, other employees, or the DOL in connection with an audit or investigation into LCA compliance (see Chapter 9).

The contents of the public access file (aka *LCA file*) will include:

1. The *signed original LCA*. Although the LCA is filed electronically, it can be printed and signed. We recommend signing in blue ink so it is clear that the document is an original and not a photocopy.

2. The documents that establish the *Prevailing Wage* (discussed in more detail in Chapter 8). Those documents typically will consist of a salary survey or a salary determination from the state job office, and a memo or chart that demonstrates why the salary chosen is appropriate for the job.

3. The *two LCA notices* (with a notation as to the locations and dates of posting).

4. The *Actual Wage Memorandum*.

The LCA file must be kept for the entire period that the employee is in H-1B status, plus one additional year.

 Filing Fees

Because of necessary cost controls, many companies, especially larger ones, have lengthy procedures for cutting checks and getting them signed. Indeed, obtaining the filing fee checks can be a delaying factor, even if you are diligent about completing the LCA process and preparing the H-1B petition. It is therefore a good idea to start the process of obtaining the filing fee checks as soon as you start the H-1B process. Do not have the check prepared too early, though, because USCIS will reject any case if the check is more than six months old at the time of filing (with potentially disastrous results if you are filing for a limited quota slot).

All checks should be made payable to "US Department of Homeland Security." There are different fees to be paid, and the best practice is to prepare separate checks for the different fees in order to avoid confusion (even though the basic fee and the training fee can be combined in one check).

The amount you must pay will vary from case to case. This section will help you determine what checks you should obtain and the likely amounts.

✹ Basic Fee

A basic fee of $325 must accompany *all* H-1B petitions, regardless of the circumstances, so a check for that amount must be prepared in all cases.

For most cases, however, the basic fee is just the beginning, and the total amount could be thousands of dollars. Before the 21st century, all H-1B cases could be filed for the same fee of $110, and those of us who have been practicing immigration law for a long time may at times grow somewhat nostalgic when confronted with today's top filing fee of $3,550.

✹ Training Fee

The training fee is collected to build a fund for the training of American workers, a practice that arose from the fanciful notion of the US Congress that sufficient training under the auspices of another government bureaucracy would obviate the need for importing H-1B professionals.

The amount of the training fee depends on the size of the company seeking to employ the H-1B worker: those with more than 25 full-time US employees must pay $1,500, and those with fewer than 26 employees must pay $750.

The training fee must be paid both with the first H-1B petition an employer files for an individual and with the first extension. The training fee is not required for second and subsequent extensions, and certain employers are exempt from the training fee altogether. One of the forms that must be submitted with every H-1B petition is the *Data Collection and Filing Fee Exemption Supplement,*[7] which, among other things, indicates whether the petition is exempt from the training fee.

❧ Is It the First or Second Extension?

The training fee is clearly required when an H-1B petition is filed for a worker who is already in H-1B status (i.e., a transfer from another US company). However, it is unclear whether the fee is required when the employer later applies to extend the H-1B status (e.g., after three years). Arguably, it is the second extension, because the first petition requested extension of the H-1B status of a person who was already in H-1B status. Apparently, USCIS does not agree with this interpretation, even though it follows a plain reading of the regulation, and even though USCIS has never issued an additional regulation or memo to clarify its policy.

It seems to be the view of many USCIS employees that each employer must pay the training fee twice (with the first two H-1B petitions submitted for each employee) regardless of whether the employee was already in H-1B status (in which case we think the employer's first H-1B petition reasonably can be regarded as an extension). We regularly submit such extension petitions without the training fee, claiming that it is the employer's second extension. In some cases, the filing fees are accepted; in others, USCIS will ask for the training fee as well. For $1,500, it seems worth the gamble in most cases.

❧ Exemptions for Certain Employers

Some employers are exempt from paying the training fee, regardless of whether it is the initial H-1B petition or the first extension. Those employers are:

- Colleges and universities

- Nonprofit organizations *affiliated* with colleges and universities

- Nonprofit research organizations and government research organizations

---

[7] www.uscis.gov/files/form/i-907.pdf

- Primary and secondard schools

- A nonprofit entity that provides traning to students

🐿 "Fraud" Fee

All initial H-1B petitions must be accompanied by a $500 fraud fee. This fee is used to fund the investigations and prosecutions described in Chapter 9 (which is another reason why it is important to prepare the H-1B carefully and truthfully!). The fraud fee is required of *all* employers, even those exempt from the H-1B quota and from the training fee. It is required only for the first H-1B petition for a particular employee and is never required for subsequent extension petitions.

🐿 Premium Processing Fee

For an additional $1,225, USCIS will expedite the H-1B petition in 15 days or less (compared with a normal processing time of 4–5 months). The request for *Premium Processing* (and the additional fee) can be submitted with the H-1B petition or later when the H-1B is pending (and you are getting tired of waiting for a response). The Premium Processing fee is always accompanied by **Form I-907.**[8]

The Premium Processing fee is overused, in our view, and US employers waste millions of dollars each year to pay for fast H-1B processing when it is not really needed.

Premium Processing is **not** normally needed:

- For an initial H-1B petition, because those typically will be filed on April 1 for an October 1 start date (see Chapter 3). The 4- to 5-month processing time normally will be subsumed within the 6 months that you must wait in any event.

⇨ **Note** A request for Premium Processing can be submitted either with the H-1B petition when it is filed, or at any time after it is filed.

- For an extension of H-1B status, because the extension petition can be submitted 6 months in advance of expiration. In addition, the employee continues to be authorized to work

---

[8] www.uscis.gov/files/forms/i-907.pdf

even if the H-1B expires, as long as the extension petition is filed before the expiration. For example, if the initial H-1B petition and status expire on June 5, and the extension petition is filed (i.e., received by USCIS) on June 4, the employee continues to be authorized to work until the extension petition is approved, even if it is not approved until October 15. When the extension petition is approved, it will be retroactive to the previous expiration date, so the employee will continuously maintain H-1B status. The only time Premium Processing makes sense in an extension petition is when the employee needs to travel internationally right away, and during the trip wishes to seek a new H-1B visa at a US embassy or consulate abroad.

- When an employee is already in H-1B status and is transferring from another company. In that case (as discussed more fully in Chapter 10), the employee is eligible to begin the employment as soon as the petition is filed and does not need to wait for approval.

There are some situations in which you will want to use Premium Processing, particularly when the employee is in another nonimmigrant status in the United States and is changing to H-1B status. For example, a person in H-4 status cannot begin H-1B employment until the petition is approved, so Premium Processing almost always should be used in that situation.

Premium Processing also should be used when the prospective employee who is outside of the United States worked previously in H-1B status for a US employer and was already counted against the H-1B quota. In that case, the employee can begin working as soon as the H-1B petition is approved and a visa secured.

 # Technology Export Control

USCIS requires all employers filing H-1B petitions to certify that they have reviewed the ***Export Administration Regulations*** (**EAR**) and ***International Traffic in Arms Regulations*** (**ITAR**) to ascertain whether an export control license is required to release the employer's technology to the H-1B employee. The certification is contained on page 5 of **Form I-129**.[9]

Normally we think of controlling technology and arms exports to foreign countries in terms of physical items, such as computer chips or missiles.

---

[9] www.uscis.gov/files/form/i-129.pdf

However, the US export controls also extend to giving technical information to foreign persons, particularly those from certain countries. Controlled technology can be found in various industries, not only in the defense industry, but also in biotechnology, chemistry, robotics, computer security, materials, and imaging.

EAR regulations can be found at:

www.bis.doc.gov/policiesandregulations/ear/index.htm.

ITAR regulations can be found at:

www.pmddtc.state.gov/regulations_laws/itar.html.

For most employers, such as those that employ IT workers to develop business and consumer applications and systems, a cursory review of the EAR and ITAR rules will be sufficient to certify this section of Form I-129. However, if there is any doubt as to the applicability of the rules, a more careful study is required to make sure that hiring the H-1B employee does not violate them.

An easy export control primer can be found on the Bureau of Industry and Security website at:

www.bis.doc.gov/seminarsandtraining/training-modules/essentials_of_export_controls_modules_1_6.pdf.

Before Form I-129 is signed, this primer should be reviewed by a person knowledgeable about the company's technology, products, and services.

Reviewing and Signing Forms and Letter

Most H-1B employers have attorneys who will prepare the H-1B forms and the supporting letter based on the information and documents gathered from both the employer and the employee. It is important that an employer representative review all of the statements and information carefully, to make sure they are accurate, before signing the documents or giving them to a company manager to sign. In particular, attention should be paid to the job description and job requirements, to make sure they have been accurately incorporated into the supporting letter. Attention should also be paid to the location of employment, and the person reviewing the case should make sure that an LCA has been obtained for each place the employee is to work.

Components of the H-1B Petition

The essential H-1B petition will assemble all of the information and documents discussed above, and will consist of the following:

- Filing fee checks

- Designation of the immigration attorney (Form G-28)

- Premium Processing form, if necessary (Form I-907)

- The H-1B petition form (Form I-129 with H Supplement)

- Filing Fee Exemption Supplement (part of Form I-129)

- Labor Condition Application (Form ETA 9035)

- Letter explaining the company, the job, and the employee's background

- Documents, such as an annual report, that demonstrate the company's existence and describe its size, revenue, products, and services

- Documents such as college degrees and transcripts that attest to the employee's academic and professional background

Responding to a Request for Evidence (RFE) or Notice of Intent to Deny (NOID)

Normally, the employer's inputs into the process end with the filing of the H-1B petition, and the next event is petition approval. However, in some cases, and with increasing frequency, USCIS will issue a *Request for Evidence* *(RFE)* that asks for additional information and documents.

Typically, the RFE will query whether the job offered is really a professional position, whether the company is sound and has the resources to hire the employee, and whether the employer is actually in charge of the employee at client locations or other remote sites where the employee may work.

USCIS can set a time in which to respond to the RFE between 30 days and 12 weeks, depending on what is reasonable for obtaining the additional information and documents.[10] For example, it may ask for a response in 12 weeks if documents from overseas must be obtained. We have found, though, that in most H-1B cases, USCIS limits the time to respond to 45 days.

In some cases, it may be possible to obtain an extension of the time in which to respond to the RFE. However, the amount of time for responding to the RFE cannot exceed 12 weeks.

A Notice of Intent to Deny (**NOID**) is rare in H-1B cases (normally an RFE is issued if there is a question about eligibility). A NOID usually means that USCIS intends to deny the petition no matter what you do. The time in which to respond to a NOID cannot exceed 30 days.

🦅 Appeals and Motions to Reconsider

Administrative appeals from H-1B denials are a cruel joke. They were probably not intended to be, but that is how they have evolved through bureaucratic mismanagement and inefficiency. An entire government office within the USCIS, the *Administrative Appeals Office* (**AAO**), has been set up to consider H-1B denials that employers believe to be wrongly decided. However—and this is the joke part—it takes one to two years to get a decision. (See the AAO processing times, attached as Appendix 6-1. The "12 months" listed is optimistic; the actual time is closer to two years. Moreover, the official process does not start until the AAO has actually received the H-1B file, which is normally several months after the appeal is filed.) Very few employers can wait that long for an employee to start or return to employment.

Despite these unworkable AAO processing times, it still can make sense to file an appeal. That is because the USCIS office ("Service Center") that denied the H-1B petition will review its denial before sending the case to the AAO. If the employer can persuade USCIS—by submitting additional evidence and perhaps legal arguments—that the case was wrongly decided, it will reverse its own decision. Often that process will take two to three months—still a long delay but worthwhile if the H-1B petition is approved.

An administrative appeal or motion to reconsider a denied H-1B petition must be submitted within 30 days of the date of the denial decision on Form I-290B.[11] This form and additional evidence or legal arguments in support of the appeal are submitted to the USCIS Service Center that denied the H-1B petition. You will know that your request for reconsideration has been successful if the Service Center reopens and approves the petition. However,

---

[10] To see a USCIS memo regarding RFE guidelines, go to www.uscis.gov/ilink/docView/FR/ HTML/FR/0-0-0-1/0-0-0-123038/0-0-0-139104/0-0-0-144323.html.

[11] www.uscis.gov/files/form/i-290b.pdf

if the Service Center does not reverse its decision, it will forward the case to the AAO. You will know that the Service Center has decided to let its decision stand if you receive a **Transfer Notice** indicating that the case was forwarded to the AAO. It is the date of this Transfer Notice that starts the clock on the official AAO processing time.

⇨ **Tip** The best strategy for correcting an incorrect H-1B petition denial may be simply to file a new petition. With Premium Processing, you can get a decision within weeks, rather than the months it could take for a Motion to Reconsider, or the years it could take for an AAO appeal. However, this approach would not be helpful if the H-1B quota was open when you filed but closed by the time you received the denial. Also, if you file a second H-1B petition, you must disclose the denial of the first petition and explain (and prove through additional evidence) why the denial was improper.

✺ Notice of Intent to Revoke (NOIR)

Even after the H-1B petition is approved, and the H-1B employee is working for your company, USCIS can later revoke the petition. Before doing so, it must give the employer an opportunity to respond to the reasons for revocation. This **Notice of Intent to Revoke (NOIR)** for an approved petition is similar to the Notice of Intent to Deny (NOID) for a pending petition, discussed above.

For example, we had a case in which the employee signed a company letter with the president's signature to verify her employment in connection with her H-1B visa application at the US embassy. The forgery was discovered, and the embassy informed USCIS. USCIS issued a NOIR. However, the employer submitted evidence that the employee was actually working for the employer in accordance with the terms of the H-1B petition and LCA, and the petition was not revoked. The only reason the employee signed the employment letter herself was because of the time and inconvenience involved in getting the correct signature.

📑 **Chapter Takeaway** The employer is responsible for preparing and filing the LCA and H-1B petition, and normally the employer's inputs into the process end when the petition is filed. However, in some cases the employer must also respond to a Request for Evidence (RFE) issued by the USCIS and may appeal if the petition is denied.

Employee Inputs to the H-1B Process

The H-1B petition is solely the employer's petition. The employee does not sign any of the documents that make up the H-1B petition and is never involved in the Labor Condition Application (LCA) process. However, the employee has a key role in providing documents and information used in the H-1B petition and has the primary responsibility for securing the H-1B visa after the petition has been approved. It is important to provide information and documents that are accurate and authentic, because you risk your employer's credibility if they are not. More critically, false information or documents can make you inadmissible to the United States forever.[1]

Résumé Drafting

You have probably prepared a résumé or curriculum vitae (CV) as an essential part of your job search, but it may be useful to review and revise it for the immigration case. Normally your résumé will not (and probably should not) be submitted with the H-1B petition, but it may be helpful to the immigration attorney who prepares your case. Full descriptions of past employment are particularly helpful when they show that your previous jobs required a college degree or equivalent, implying that your H-1B job will likewise. It is helpful to

---

[1] See "A Lie Can Exclude You from the United States Forever" at www.immilaw.com/ Newsletters/2007%20January%20Lies%20and%20Waivers.htm.

include not just your college degrees but also the dates that you attended each college or university (for example, September 2003 to May 2007). That will help the attorney determine more easily whether you have a four-year degree or a three-year degree, and therefore how the petition should be prepared.

Supporting Documentation

The documents to be submitted to the employer or the employer's attorney may vary somewhat from case to case, but an essential list includes the following:

1. Copies of all college and university degree certificates.

2. Copies of college transcripts or mark sheets that reflect the courses attended. Usually unofficial transcripts are sufficient, since the most important fact, your graduation, is proven by your college degree. We do not need secondary school documents.

3. Credential evaluation if your foreign degrees have ever been evaluated by a professional credential evaluator. If not, the employer's attorney will have them evaluated if necessary (often it will not be). If you do not already have a credential evaluation, it is not usually cost-effective, in terms of either time or money, to obtain one.

4. Résumé or CV.

5. Copy of Form I-94, "Arrival-Departure Record" (if you are already in the United States). A copy of both sides of the I-94 is required, even though the reverse side may not have any notation on it.

⇨ **Note**   The Form I-94 is currently being phased out, and by 2015 US arrivals and departures will be tracked electronically, without any hard-copy documentation except a stamp in your passport.

---

6. Copies of the passports of your accompanying spouse and children, and copies of your marriage certificate and the children's birth certificates. If they are in the United States, you must submit a copy of their Forms I-94 as well.

7. Copy of Form I-20 if you are currently in the United States in student status.

8. Copies of *all* forms DS-2019 or IAP-66 if you have *ever* been in the United States in J-1 status.

9. Copies of all previous H-1B approval forms (Form I-797).

10. Copy of the Employment Authorization Document (EAD) if you have one. (N.b. To photocopy the EAD, the photocopying machine must be on the lightest setting; otherwise the expiration date is not sufficiently clear). If the EAD card was extended, send a copy of the reverse side as well.

11. Copy of your offer letter or other contract with the employer.

12. If you are currently in H-1B status, your two most recent paycheck stubs that show that you have been recently employed by the H-1B petitioner.

⇨ **Tip** All documents can be photocopies. USCIS rarely requires original documents. However, it is a good idea to take your original degree certificates to the visa interview at the US consulate or embassy, since often the authenticity of the degree will be an issue.

Request for Evidence

Although input from the employee into the H-1B petition process usually ends after the initial submission of documents, increasingly often USCIS will issue the dreaded *Request for Evidence* (RFE). There are two ways of viewing the RFE. Optimists will see it as a further opportunity to demonstrate eligibility. Pessimists will see it as USCIS's first step toward denying the petition, issued by a USCIS examiner who is not convinced that there is eligibility.

Normally, the RFE will request information that only the employer can provide, such as evidence that the company exists, that the employment opportunity is realistic for the business, that the employer can pay the offered salary, and that the job is a professional position. Occasionally, though, the RFE will require input from the employee, such as evidence of professional background. Since the H-1B petition is solely the employer's petition, USCIS will not send any notices—including receipts, RFEs, approvals, and denials—directly to the employee. If the employer needs information from you, the employer or the employer's attorney will let you know.

⇨ **Tip** Even though the H-1B petition is the employer's petition, it affects you. Also, you will need to be familiar with the entire contents of the petition, including any RFE and response, when you apply for your visa. Do not be afraid to ask for copies of all of the documents that comprise the petition. If the immigration attorney represents you as well as the employer, you should be able to get copies of all documents from the attorney (see our discussion on dual representation in Chapter 5).

Visa Application at the US Embassy or Consulate

Once the H-1B petition is approved, you can apply for the *H-1B visa*—which is a stamp in your passport that entitles you to enter the United States. The visa is only that—an entry document—and your actual status in the United States is governed by the Form I-94 that Customs and Border Protection (CBP) will give you upon entry (see below).

⇨ **Canada Exception** Canadian citizens do not need a visa. Instead, you can enter the US with just your unexpired Canadian passport, a copy of the H-1B approval notice (Form I-797), and a copy of the H-1B petition.

The visa application has three primary parts: paying the visa fee ($190 in 2013); completing the online visa application; and scheduling an interview.

The first step will be to determine at which US embassy or consulate you will apply. Normally, that will be the US embassy or consulate closest to your place of residence in your home country. However, that is not always the case: for example, citizens of Belarus can apply for their visas in Moscow. Also, there is no law against applying at any US embassy or consulate in the world, although most will discourage you from applying outside of your home district (and may send you back to the US embassy or consulate closest to where you normally live). The US State Department does not want applicants to shop around for the fastest or easiest place to apply (otherwise, a visa-issuing post with a reputation for fast processing times and a friendly staff might be overwhelmed by more applications than it could handle). However, if you are living near a US consulate outside of your home country or have a very good reason for applying there, the consulate probably will not turn you away. For example, if you normally live close to the US Consulate in Chennai, India, but are temporarily working in the United Kingdom, you can apply for your visa in London.

Once you have determined where you will apply, you should review carefully the application procedures on the website of the US embassy or consulate. Each visa-issuing post has its own unique procedures and requirements, so it is important to study those carefully. Links to all US embassies and consulates in the world can be found at http://www.usembassy.gov/. At the top of each home page is a "Visas" button, which will take you to the instructions for applying for "nonimmigrant visas" (some have more specific instructions for applying for H-1B visas). Those instructions will direct you to a payment center (usually a bank or online) to pay the visa fee.

India Exception The US Embassy and Consulates in India do not handle the visa application process in-house but have centralized that function through a web portal at http://www.ustraveldocs.com/in/.

You will also need to submit a passport-size photograph and complete the online visa application form (*Form DS-160*[2]). This form is extremely unwieldy and user-unfriendly and requires navigating through many pages without the ability to save your work (leading to the vexing risk of losing all of your work and having to start over).

In addition to gathering biographical data about you, this form seeks to determine whether you are "inadmissible" to the US. There are many grounds of inadmissibility, including prior criminal activity, previous US immigration violations, and serious health problems. It is important to consider your answers carefully, since a misrepresentation can provide a further ground of inadmissibility. If you have any doubts about your admissibility, you should review those issues with the immigration attorney. If a ground of inadmissibility does apply to you (for example, if you previously had a minor conviction for selling marijuana), a waiver of inadmissibility may be possible.

---

[2] https://ceac.state.gov/genniv/

💣 **Caution**   One trap for the unwary on Form DS-160 is the question, "Have you ever been refused a US visa?" Often a visa application will not be granted, because the application was not submitted with sufficient evidence. For example, a visitor's visa application might not be granted because the applicant could not demonstrate sufficient ties to his or her home country. In that case, the applicant might be invited to apply again later. Since the visa was not formally denied, just rejected for lack of evidence, a person might logically believe that it was not a visa "refusal". However, the US consular officer might conclude that answering "no" to that question amounts to a misrepresentation (and therefore a reason to deny the H-1B visa).

⇨ **Note**   H-1B visa applicants are *not* required to demonstrate sufficient ties to their home countries.

The final part of the visa-issuing process is the interview at the US embassy or consulate. Normally that interview will be very short—probably just a few minutes after an hour's wait—but the consular official may have some questions about your professional degrees and the nature of the proposed employment in the United States. Some US consulates, such as those in India, may require further evidence about the employer, so for those visa-issuing posts it is a good idea to bring evidence in addition to the documents submitted with the H-1B petition. That evidence might include the company's annual report or a recent letter confirming that the job offer is still available.

Most visas are issued for the same period as the H-1B approval notice (Form I-797), which is normally three years. However, nationals of some countries—such as China, Mexico, and Russia—are limited to a period of only one or two years of H-1B visa validity. Also, nationals of some countries—such as China—are limited to a single entry for each H-1B visa (which means that you would have to obtain a new H-1B visa at the US embassy or consulate every time you travel).

⇨ **Tip**   You can determine the maximum period of H-1B eligibility for nationals of your country, and whether the H-1B visa is issued for multiple entries, from the US State Department's "Country Reciprocity Schedule" at http://travel.state.gov/visa/fees/fees_3272.html.

For those who previously had an H-1B visa and seek to renew it, an interview might not be necessary. Instead, you can submit your passport, and the US embassy or consulate will return it with the H-1B visa.

Entry into the United States

Now that you have your H-1B visa, you are almost done. You can travel to the US and start your employment. You have one final step in the process: to get through the immigration inspection at the international airport or border when you arrive in the US.

⇨ **Note**   At international airports in Canada (such as in Vancouver, Toronto, and Montreal) and in London and Dublin, the immigration inspection is conducted before individuals arrive in the United States,.

Immigration inspection is conducted by US Customs and Border Protection. Normally, you will present three documents to pass inspection:

1.   Your unexpired passport containing your H-1B visa.

2.   A copy of the H-1B approval notice (Form I-797).

3.   Evidence that the H-1B employment is still available. That can be a letter from the employer confirming the job offer or, if the H-1B petition was submitted recently, a copy of the employer's letter that accompanied the petition. If you are already working for the employer in H-1B status, a recent paycheck stub with the employer's and your name on it should be sufficient.

It is a good idea also to have with you a complete copy of the H-1B petition.

There are three levels of inspection. Normally the first level is at the CBP window at the international airport after you have disembarked and collected your luggage. At this level, the CBP officer will inspect your documents and ask for a single fingerprint. Ideally, the process should take only a couple of minutes. However, if there are any questions about your eligibility to enter the US, you will be taken to another room for secondary inspection.

Secondary inspection can take several hours, which can be quite daunting at the end of an overseas flight. However, it is important to maintain your composure and be polite to the CBP officer. It is even more important to tell the truth (any intentional misrepresentation could lead to your permanent expulsion from the US). The CBP inspector may wish to inquire into whether your job offer is real and whether you have any past history of US immigration violations or criminal activity that could affect your right to enter the US. It is even possible that your name and birth date are the same as those of a terrorist or criminal, and there is confusion about your identity.

⇨ **Tip** If your name is on a watch list and you experience problems passing through immigration inspections, you may be able to clear your name by contacting the Department of Homeland Security (DHS) at its web portal at http://www.dhs.gov/dhs-trip.

There is also a third level of inspection possible, called "deferred inspection." In that case, you will be allowed to enter the US and to leave the airport, but you will not be formally "admitted" into the US. Instead, you will be asked to return later to the airport or to a CBP office to complete the admission process. Normally, deferred inspections are scheduled when it is not really clear whether you should be admitted into the US, and additional information is needed to make that determination. For example, if there is a question as to whether the H-1B employment is still available, the CBP inspector may ask you to appear for deferred inspection to prove that it is. CBP may allow an attorney to accompany you to deferred inspection.

⇨ **Tip** The H-1B regulations make it clear that you should be admitted into the US until the expiration date on the *H-1B approval notice* (Form I-797) (unless your passport expires before then). However, many CBP officers are unaware of this rule and may want to admit you only until the expiration date of your *H-1B visa*. In that case, you should politely remind the CBP office that you "shall be admitted to the United States for the validity period of the petition" and perhaps ask to speak to a supervisor if the inspector that you talk to insists on limiting your admission to the visa expiration date, rather than the petition expiration date. If you need to refer the CBP officer to this rule, you can mention 8 CFR 214.2(h)(13)(i)(A).

Labor Condition Application (LCA) Compliance

On its surface, the Labor Condition Application (LCA) process appears to be simple: it is meant to ensure that the employer pays a salary and benefits that are high enough that they do not undercut the salaries and benefits of American professionals generally or of other employees of your company.

However, because of the various political compromises made in their formation, the LCA rules are incredibly complex and convoluted and hide pitfalls for the unwary. Fines, payment of back wages, battles with the Department of Labor, and exclusion from the H-1B program await employers who do not abide by these byzantine rules (see Chapter 9).

The Required Wage

The key to LCA compliance is paying the H-1B employee a sufficient salary. If this is done, a minor violation of the other LCA requirements might not result in significant penalties. This minimum salary is referred to in the regulations as the **Required Wage**.

The Required Wage is the higher of two different numbers: the *Prevailing Wage* and the *Actual Wage*.

The Prevailing Wage

The **Prevailing Wage** is the average salary of other people doing similar work as the H-1B employee. Specifically, it is the weighted average salary for the specific occupational classification paid by all employers in the geographic area of intended employment. For example, the Prevailing Wage for Perry County, Alabama, will not be applicable for employment in the Borough of Manhattan, New York.

Therefore, the factors to consider in determining the Prevailing Wage are:

- **Location of employment.** Normally that refers to the *county* in which the work will occur, and the comparison is with other workers in that county.

- **Occupational category.** The Department of Labor (DOL) divides all occupations into discrete categories and assigns a number to each. There is of course some overlap between categories (for example, Computer Systems Analyst, Programmer, and Applications Software Developer), but it is important to try to find the closest match to the job offered. Those occupational categories can be found on the O*NET website at www.onetonline.org/.

- **Level.** Obviously, the salaries of entry-level workers should not be compared with those of supervisors in the same occupational category. The Prevailing Wage must be based on education, experience, and other requirements for the job.

It is important to apply these factors accurately and in good faith. If you do not (if, for example, you falsely claim that an experienced worker will be in an entry-level job), you risk incurring your company's liability for LCA violations (discussed in Chapter 9).

✺ Primary Sources for Determining the Prevailing Wage

DOL regulations provide several different methods for determining the Prevailing Wage, but only one—described in the next section—provides a "safe harbor" in the event of a later audit.

DOL Prevailing Wage Determination

"Safe harbor" in the event of an audit can be preemptively secured by obtaining a *Prevailing Wage Determination* (PWD) directly from the DOL. Information about the employer, job duties, management responsibilities, education requirements, experience requirements, special requirements, and travel requirements are provided online to the DOL through its *iCERT* portal (at http://icert.doleta.gov/). The DOL will issue a wage determination within 60 days or so. As long as the information provided is accurate, and the employer actually pays that salary, the employer is insulated from liability for failing to pay the Prevailing Wage (although it might still have liability for failing to pay the Actual Wage, described in the "Actual Wage" section below).

💣 **Caution**   The problem with using a PWD obtained through iCERT is that it normally takes too long, especially for new hires. Most employers cannot afford to wait two months (or even two weeks) to determine the Prevailing Wage. The goal in most cases is to get the H-1B petition approved as quickly as possible. For that reason, we rarely recommend using the DOL PWD, even though the employer would not enjoy complete protection from liability in the event that the proper Prevailing Wage was not paid to the H-1B employee.

✺ Department of Labor Online Wage Survey

Instead of the DOL specific determination, we normally recommend using the same salary survey that the DOL uses when it issues a PWD through iCERT. That salary survey can be found on another DOL website, the Online Wage Library: www.flcdatacenter.com/OesWizardStart.aspx.

Directly using this OES Prevailing Wage guidance (rather than getting an individualized determination from the DOL) does not provide complete protection from liability, but it comes pretty close—especially if care is taken to make sure that (1) the correct occupational category is chosen, and (2) the correct "level" is chosen.

This Online Wage Library provides summary descriptions of the various occupational categories, and normally those will be sufficient to determine the correct occupational category. However, if there is any doubt, you should review the more complete descriptions of the occupations on the O*NET website (www.onetonline.org/). If two occupational categories are both arguably correct for the H-1B position (for example, computer systems analyst and applications software developer), it may be a good idea to add a memo to the LCA file that explains why you believe the category you picked is more appropriate.

OES salaries are divided into four skill levels, depending on the requirements of the job. Level 1 is for an entry-level position that normally requires no or little prior experience. Level 4 is applied to positions that require more experience than normal.

Assignment to one of the four levels depends on the amount of education and experience the DOL believes is a normal requirement for the job. This normal requirement is referred to as the *Specific Vocational Preparation* (**SVP**), which for many professional positions is a bachelor's degree plus two to four years of experience (designated as an SVP of 7 to < 8) (see Appendix 8-1). In that case, a job that requires two to three years of experience would be assigned to Level 2, one that requires three to four years of experience would be assigned to Level 3, and one that requires over four years of experience would be assigned to Level 4.

A level must be added if the job normally requires a bachelor's degree, but the particular H-1B job requires a master's degree. Two levels must be added if the job requires a PhD, unless a PhD is the normal requirement for the occupation, such as for a Computer Research Scientist. A level is added for a foreign language requirement, supervisory responsibilities, or a special certificate or license (such as a Microsoft Certified IT Professional certification). As you can see, it is easy to get to Level 4, the highest Prevailing Wage, very quickly.

A DOL guide to determining the proper OES salary level is reproduced in Appendix 8-2. A worksheet to use with the salary guide is reproduced in Appendix 8-3.

In addition to these mechanical measures for comparing the SVP to the H-1B employer's own job requirements, the DOL provides the following guidance for determining the proper job level:

- **Level 1 (entry)** wage rates are assigned to job offers for beginning-level employees who have only a basic understanding of the occupation. These employees perform routine tasks that require limited, if any, exercise of judgment. The tasks provide experience and familiarization with the employer's methods, practices, and programs. The employees may perform higher-level work for training and developmental purposes. These employees work under close supervision and receive specific instructions on required tasks and results expected. Their work is closely monitored and reviewed for accuracy. Statements that the job offer is for a research fellow, a worker in training, or an internship are indicators that a Level I wage should be considered.

- **Level 2 (qualified)** wage rates are assigned to job offers for qualified employees who have attained, through either education or experience, a good understanding of the occupation. They perform moderately complex tasks that require limited judgment. An indicator that the job request warrants a wage determination at Level 2 would be a requirement for years of education and/or experience that are generally required as particularized in the O*NET Job Zones.

- **Level 3 (experienced)** wage rates are assigned to job offers for experienced employees who have a sound understanding of the occupation and have attained, through either education or experience, special skills or knowledge. They perform tasks that require exercising judgment and may coordinate the activities of other staff. They may have supervisory authority over those staff. A requirement for years of experience or educational degrees that are at the higher ranges indicated in the O*NET Job Zones would be indicators that a Level 3 wage should be considered.

  Frequently, key words in the job title can be used as indicators that an employer's job offer is for an experienced worker. Words such as lead (as in "lead analyst"), senior ("senior programmer"), head ("head nurse"), chief ("crew chief"), or journeyman ("journeyman plumber") would be indicators that a Level 3 wage should be considered.

- **Level 4 (fully competent)** wage rates are assigned to job offers for competent employees who have sufficient experience in the occupation to plan and conduct work requiring judgment and the independent evaluation, selection, modification, and application of standard procedures and techniques. Such employees use advanced skills and diversified knowledge to solve unusual and complex problems. These employees receive only technical guidance and their work is reviewed only for application of sound judgment and effectiveness in meeting the establishment's procedures and expectations. They generally have management and/or supervisory responsibilities.

It might be helpful to quote this DOL language in the memo that you will place in the LCA file explaining why you believe you chose the proper level.

By carefully documenting your reasoning in choosing the occupational category, and the proper salary level within that occupation, you are able to cite a Prevailing Wage source that is almost as good as a Prevailing Wage determination, without the expensive delay involved in ordering a PWD.

🖎 Private Sources for Determining the Prevailing Wage

The employer also has the option of using a private salary survey (rather than the OES government survey). That can be either a commercial survey provided by a company like Radford or Watson Wyatt, or the employer's own survey. To be acceptable, the survey must meet the following criteria:

• It has been published within 24 months of the date of submission of the Prevailing Wage request

• It is the most current edition of the survey

• It is based on data collected within 24 months of the date of the publication of the survey

Normally, Radford requires an expensive subscription to gain access to its salary surveys (e.g., the Radford Global Technology Survey), but custom surveys for nonsubscribers may be available as well. Many large technology companies already subscribe to Radford to help determine competitive salaries.

In a later LCA audit, if there is one, the DOL may not consider the Radford or other private survey to be as authoritative as the OES (DOL online) survey, and it is certainly more cumbersome to use. It therefore should be used only when the OES salary result seems too high and is inappropriate based on the employer's understanding of current industry conditions, and when the salary reflected in the private salary survey is lower.

When using the private salary survey, it is important to fully document in the LCA file the adequacy of the survey. At a minimum, such documentation should include a copy of the weighted average salaries for the various levels, the leveling guidelines, the occupational description, the survey data size, the geographical boundaries of the survey, and the survey methodology. DOL guidelines describing the specific requirements are reproduced in Appendix 8-4.

❧ The Actual Wage

The other component of the Required Wage is the **Actual Wage**. That is the amount *paid by the employer to other employees* who:

1. Do work similar to that done by the H-1B employee, and

2. Work at the same location, and

3. Have similar education, experience, and other qualifications.

The employer must document, in an **Actual Wage Memorandum** placed in the LCA file, that the H-1B employee earns the same as or more than all other similarly employed workers at the same location, or that there is a good reason why she does not. That may require making a list of all other employees in a similar position and explaining why the H-1B employee will earn less. For example:

> *ABC Corporation employs 16 software engineers in Northern California, with salaries that range from $75,000 to $130,000. Only three of these engineers earn more than the $115,000 salary offered to the H-1B Employee. Employee A earns $120,000 but has two more years of experience than the H-1B Employee, as well as having a master's degree, which the H-1B Employee does not have. Employee B earns $130,000 but is the primary software architect and has project leadership responsibilities. In contrast, the H-1B Employee will not be involved in a role that determines the direction of our software development and will not have any managerial duties.*

If the H-1B employee is offered a salary at the top of the range, then preparing the Actual Wage Memorandum becomes much easier:

> *ABC Corporation employs 16 software engineers in Northern California, with salaries that range from $75,000 to $130,000. The H-1B Employee will be paid $130,000, which therefore equals or exceeds the Actual Wage.*

If there are no similarly employed workers, the Actual Wage Memorandum becomes even easier:

> *The H-1B Employee will be the only software engineer employed by ABC Corporation. Her offered salary of $75,000 is therefore the Actual Wage.*

(Of course, you must also make sure that the offered salary equals or exceeds the Prevailing Wage, as discussed in the preceding section.)

There is a question as to whether an existing employee's longevity at the company can be a factor in determining the Actual Wage. We believe that in some cases, longevity can be an important factor. For example:

> *ABC Corporation employs one other software engineer who will earn more than the H-1B Employee. Just like the H-1B employee, that other software engineer has a bachelor's degree in computer science and five years of experience. That other software engineer earns $130,000, $15,000 per year more than the $115,000 offered to the H-1B Employee. However, the other software engineer has already been working for ABC Corporation for three years and is intimately familiar with ABC Corporation's development environment and cutting-edge technology. The H-1B Employee is not familiar with ABC Corporation's proprietary technology, and it will take several years for him to develop this expertise.*

However, in a later audit, the DOL may not agree with this approach, so other reasons, if any, for the salary discrepancy should be explained as well. Specifically, the regulations provide that the following factors may be considered in determining the Actual Wage:

- Experience
- Qualifications
- Education
- Job responsibility and function
- Specialized knowledge
- "Other legitimate business factors"

An H-1B employee's prior experience with the same employer might be considered a "legitimate business factor" or it might be considered to undermine the purpose of the Actual Wage altogether. Whether or not the DOL finds that factor to be reasonable may turn on the persuasiveness of your explanation in the Actual Wage Memorandum.

Regulations require that the Actual Wage Memorandum must be detailed enough to enable a third party to "understand how the employer applied its pay system to arrive at the Actual Wage for its H-1B nonimmigrant(s)."

Ultimately, whether you have accurately determined the Actual Wage will depend on its essential purpose: to make sure that you treat the H-1B employee in the same manner you would a US employee, and that the salary paid is consistent with the salaries paid to existing employees.

🔖 **Takeaway**   The *Actual Wage Memorandum* must state the wage to be paid to the H-1B employee and describe how it is consistent with the wages paid to other employees of the company who have similar backgrounds and jobs.

⚜ When the Required Wage Must Be Paid

The Required Wage (the higher of the Actual Wage and Prevailing Wage) must be paid from the time the H-1B employee begins the employment and must continue until the proper termination of employment. Moreover, the Required Wage must be paid even if the employee is not yet working for the employer, beginning 30 days after the employee arrives in the United States in H-1B status. If the employee is already in the United States, the obligation to pay begins the later of (1) 60 days after the H-1B petition is approved or (2) the start date on the petition, regardless of whether the employee has begun working for the employer.

This obligation to pay the employee continues even if there is no work available, and the employment must be suspended by the employer (*benching*). That means if the employee is underemployed, the only recourse to stop paying the Required Wage is (1) to properly terminate the employee or (2) to file an amended H-1B petition to reflect a part-time employment status.

However, payment of the Required Wage can be suspended if the H-1B employee requests a temporary absence from work—for example, for a maternity leave, sickness, or vacation. In that case, it is a good idea to get an email, letter, memo, or other acknowledgment from the employee confirming that it is the employee's decision to stop working temporarily.

⚜ How the Required Wage Must Be Paid

The Required Wage must be paid on a regular payroll with payroll taxes deducted and reported to the Internal Revenue Service (IRS). The employee may *not* be paid as an independent contractor with reporting on Form 1099. The salary must be paid at least monthly, although there is an exception for schools that do not pay salaries during summer vacations. The Required Wage cannot be in the form of bonuses or commissions, and it cannot be paid irregularly (that is, the salary must be prorated evenly over each pay period).

Generally, there can be no payroll deductions that would make the salary dip below the Required Wage, with the following exceptions:

- Deductions required by law, including federal income tax, state income tax, and FICA taxes

- Union dues

- Health insurance premiums

- Retirement fund contribution

- Wage garnishment (up to 25% of disposable earnings)

- Other deductions authorized in writing that are principally for the benefit of the H-1B employee (such as repayment of a loan)

Deductions may *not* include any H-1B expenses or any other employer business expenses, such as for tools and equipment, or travel expenses for travel required by the employer.

Employee Payment of H-1B Fees and Costs

The DOL considers all costs associated with the H-1B petition, including the legal fees and filing fees, to be properly attributed to the employer. Whether it is acceptable for the employee ever to pay any of these fees and costs is a matter of debate and speculation. So far, the DOL has not issued any clear policy guidance that resolves the matter one way or the other.

DOL rules are clear that the employee may not pay any of the training fee ($1,500 for employers with more than 25 full-time employees or $750 for those with less).

However, the employee may be able to pay other filing fees and perhaps the legal fees as well.

We include this discussion of who must pay the H-1B costs in this section on the Required Wage because payment of H-1B costs may affect the payment of the Required Wage. Since the DOL considers those costs to be properly attributed to the employer, payment of any of these costs by the employee reduces the employee's net pay.

If the salary offered the employee exceeds the Required Wage, the employee should be able to pay those costs (or at least the amount by which the actual salary exceeds the Required Wage). On the other hand, the employee may not pay the attorney's fee or other costs related to the H-1B petition if paying those fees and costs would cause the employee's net wage to dip below the Required Wage. For example, if the Required Wage is $75,000, the employee earns $77,000, and the H-1B legal fee is $3,000, by paying the legal fee the employee would end up with a net salary of $74,000, an amount below the Required Wage. The DOL probably would consider that an LCA violation.

Takeaway   The LCA regulations do not expressly prohibit the employee from paying the legal fees and costs of the H-1B petition, with the sole exception of the training fee. However, the Department of Labor may not agree, and it has not provided specific guidance. The most conservative approach (to avoid the possibility of incurring fines or other penalties associated with this matter) is for the employer to pay *all* H-1B legal fees and costs.

LCA Notice Posting Requirements

Before the LCA can be filed with the Department of Labor, LCA notices must be posted in two places at each location where the employee is expected to work. The notices must be up for 10 days. However, you do not have to wait the 10 days before filing the LCA but can file it as soon as the notices are posted. The regulations provide the following guidance regarding acceptable posting locations:

> *The notice shall be clearly visible and unobstructed while posted and shall be posted in conspicuous places, where the employer's U.S. workers can readily read the posted notice on their way to or from their place of employment. Appropriate locations for posting notices of the job opportunity include, but are not limited to, locations in the immediate vicinity of the wage and hour notices . . . or occupational safety and health notices . . .*

The content of the LCA notices will mirror the content of the LCA. At a minimum, the notices must include the following:

- The number of H-1B employees the employer is seeking under the corresponding LCA

- The occupational classification based on the DOL occupational codes (which can be found on the O*NET website, www.onetonline.org/)

- The wages offered

- The period of employment
- The address where the H-1B worker or workers will be employed

In addition, the LCA notices must include the following statement:

> *Complaints alleging misrepresentation of matrial facts in the Labor Condition Application and/or failure to comply with the terms of the Labor Condition Application may be filed with any office of the Wage and Hour Division of the United States Department of Labor.*

Appropriate places for posting may include a break room, in the lobby of the building through which employees pass on their way to their workstations, or on the company bulletin board. You must find two such appropriate places, post the LCA notices, calendar to make sure the notices are up for 10 days, and write the locations and dates of posting on the notices (for example, "bulletin board in kitchen, 2/3/13 to 2/13/13"). Those notices will then be placed in the LCA file.

In the alternative, the LCA notices can be sent to all other employees in the same occupation by email or by posting on the company intranet.

If the employee is to work at a client site, notice must be given either by posting the LCA notice at the client site or by providing notice by email or intranet to the employees at your company *and at the client's company*. That is one reason it can be logistically difficult to place H-1B employees at client sites for long periods.

If the position is a union job, instead of posting the LCA notice, an employer must give notice of the LCA to the collective bargaining representative. This circumstance is very unusual, since most H-1B petitions involve positions that are not unionized. However, there are some professional positions in which membership in a union is required (for example, nurse or ship officer).

 # H-1B Dependent Employers

An employer is *H-1B dependent* if it has more than a prescribed number of H-1B employees, as follows:

Company Size	Number of H-1B Employees
25 employees or less	7
26 to 50 employees	12
More than 50 employees	15% of the workforce

H-1B dependent employers must meet onerous additional requirements, such as recruiting US workers and proving that hiring the H-1B employee will not displace US workers.

However, those additional requirements for H-1B dependent employers do *not* apply to employees who (1) have a master's degree *or* (2) will earn at least $60,000 per year. (This $60,000 figure, established in 2000, is outdated because most H-1B professionals now earn more than that.) Such H-1B employees are considered **exempt**.

Therefore, the additional requirements for H-1B dependent employers can be ignored most of the time. However, it is still important to determine whether your company is H-1B dependent, because that must be stated on the LCA. Also, a list of all exempt H-1B employees (which normally means all H-1B employees) must be included in the LCA file.

 # Formal Requirements of the LCA File

The LCA file must be kept at the location of the H-1B worker's employment or at the company's headquarters, and it must be made available to the public after the LCA has been filed. At a minimum, it must contain the following:

- The original signed LCA for each work site.

- The two LCA notices posted at each work site (or evidence that alternative methods for providing notice were used, as discussed in the preceding section).

- Documents that reflect how the Prevailing Wage was determined. Typically, those will include a copy of the OES Online Wage Library printout, the Skill Level Worksheet (reproduced in Appendix 8-3), and any other documents that establish that the occupational category and skill level were correctly determined.

- The Actual Wage Memorandum (discussed in the "Actual Wage" section above).

- A summary of the benefits (such as health insurance and pension benefits) offered to employees in the same occupational category as the H-1B employee, and, if all employees (including the H-1B employee) will not receive the same benefits, an explanation of the reason. This summary of benefits can be included in the Actual Wage Memorandum, or in a separate document.

- A list of *exempt* H-1B employees if the employer is *H-1B dependent* (as discussed in the preceding subsection).

The regulations also require that the following documents be made available in the case of an LCA audit:

- Payroll records relating to all employees similarly employed at the same location. These payroll records must include, for each such employee, the employee's name, address, occupation, rate of pay, hours worked (if paid hourly), payroll deductions, and total wages paid each pay period.

- A copy of all documents provided to employees that describe employee benefits (such as plan summaries, employee handbooks, benefit plans, and rules for differentiating benefits among different groups of workers).

- Evidence as to what benefits are actually provided to US workers and the H-1B employee.

Employers normally maintain these types of records in any event and would not have to create them for the H-1B case. This additional documentation does not have to be, and should not be, included in the LCA file.

Employment in More Than One Location: LCA Requirement for Each Long-Term Site

In general, an H-1B employee cannot work at a new location (one not designated on the LCA) unless an LCA is filed and LCA notices are posted at that location *before* the employee begins work at that location.

This rule presents a challenge for employers who wish to place the employee at client sites for consulting assignments (as is common in the IT industry). Each long-term assignment (of 30 days or more) requires an LCA for the assigned work location (including posting of the LCA notices at that location).

Many IT companies that hire H-1B employees to work as consultants at client sites violate this requirement, because they do not want to ask their clients to post LCA notices at the work site or because they are simply unaware of the requirement. However, it is imperative to keep the following rule in mind.

Rule   The LCA and H-1B petition are specific to one location, and if the location changes new filings are required.

Moving to a Nearby Location

There are several exceptions to this rule. First, no new LCA is required if the employee moves to another location within the same "area of intended employment" (usually defined as an area that encompasses a normal commuting distance). *However, the two LCA notices must be posted at the new location* before *the employment begins.*

Two examples are instructive. To take one type of case, if the H-1B employee works at the employer's headquarters, and those offices move across the street—or across town—the same LCA notices that relate to that employee's previously approved LCA should be posted for 10 days in two conspicuous places at the new place of employment. This should be done before the employee moves to the new location. (This means that when the H-1B employee is to move with all of the other employees to the new offices at the same time, the LCA notices might be posted in an empty building!)

Another example would be an H-1B consultant who is working for the employer at a client site. If the project ends, and the employee is to work for another client at another location in the same city (that is, in the same "area of intended employment," or normal commuting distance), a new LCA is not required. However, the LCA notices that were posted at the first client site should be posted at the second client site *before* the project at the second site begins.

Exemption for Short-Term Placements of Less Than 30 Days

For assignments of less than 30 days within a one-year period in an area of intended employment, an LCA is not required, nor are LCA notices. However, in that case, the employer must pay the travel expenses (including the actual cost of lodging, transportation, meals, and "miscellaneous expenses") for both workdays and non-workdays.

A traveling consultant in H-1B status who had an LCA completed for the employer's headquarters may travel throughout the United States for implementation projects that last less than 30 days. No new LCA or posting is required as long as the employee's total time in each area of intended employment is less than 30 days within a one-year period. However, as soon as the employment in any city reaches 30 days within that period (even if the employment is not for 30 consecutive days), a new LCA must be obtained, and LCA notices must be posted.

For example, if a consultant based in Washington, DC, has a two-week project in New York City, followed by a three-week project in San Francisco, followed by a one-week project in Chicago, no new LCA or notices are required for any of these assignments. However, if the consultant returns within the year to New York City for another three-week project, an LCA and posting would be required.

⇨ **Tip**   Only one LCA is required for each "area of intended employment" (of more than 30 days within a one-year period), but LCA notices are required for each job site. The employer can obtain LCAs in advance for each metropolitan area where it expects the H-1B employee to work for more than 30 days within a one-year period, and then post the LCA notices at each job site before the project at that site begins.

❧ Exemption for Short-Term Placements between 30 and 60 Days

If certain guidelines are met, a new LCA and notices are not required for an assignment of between 30 to 60 days within an area of intended employment.

If an office or workstation is maintained for the employee at the central location for which an LCA was obtained, the 30-day limit on short-term placements is increased to 60 days per year. To be eligible for the extended 60-day short-term placement exemption, the employee must reside near the office or workstation and must spend a substantial amount of his or her time there.

❧ Exemption for Short-Term Job Sites of Less Than 6 Days or Less Than 11 Days, Depending on the Nature of the Job

The regulations also provide for an LCA exemption for an employee who is *peripatetic* (a word used in the LCA regulations, from the Greek root meaning "walking about"). A *peripatetic worker* is someone like a traveling salesperson, or perhaps a technical support engineer, who is in a job that by its nature requires frequent travel to other locations on a short-term basis. The peripatetic worker can work up to five consecutive days at other work sites, and *there is no limit to the total number of days per year that can be spent at the other worksites in the area of intended employment* (as long as each visit is five days or less). The peripatetic worker does not have a primary work site, but the initial LCA and posting should be done for the company's headquarters.

Another type of exemption is provided for an H-1B employee who spends most of his or her time at a primary work site (for which an LCA was obtained) but who occasionally visits other sites on a short-term basis. In that case, the employee can visit for up to 10 consecutive days, and like the peripatetic worker is not subject to a limit of total days visiting the site each year.

These visits to an outside location can be recurring, but they cannot be excessive. For example, an attempt to avoid LCAs, by having the employee continually move between two work sites for five days each time, would probably be viewed as a violation of the letter and spirit of the regulations and could lead to LCA penalties.

Examples of peripatetic workers (eligible to stay for five days) and short-term visitors who have a central workplace (eligible to stay for 10 days) might include a computer engineer who troubleshoots client problems on-site and an outside auditor who conducts reviews at client companies.

For a traveling consultant with longer-term assignments, compliance with the LCA requirements, including posting at each work site, can be onerous or prohibitive. These compliance requirements should be considered in planning assignments for H-1B employees, or even in deciding whether to hire such employees for those positions in the first place.

Chapter Takeaway The Required Wage—the higher of the Prevailing Wage and the Actual Wage—must be paid from the start of the H-1B employment until the employee is properly terminated. That includes periods of *benching* (i.e., when the employment is suspended), unless the employee requests leave for such things as vacation, illness, injury, or maternity leave. The basis for the Required Wage must be documented in an *LCA file*, which must be available to public access for at least one year after the H-1B employment ends. An LCA must be filed, and LCA documentation prepared, for each long-term work site.

H-1B Investigations and Penalties

Audits and investigations to ensure the integrity of the H-1B program are conducted (1) by the **Wage and Hour Division (WHD)** of the Department of Labor (to ensure compliance with the Labor Condition Application regulations) and (2) by the **Fraud Detection and National Security (FDNS)** unit of USCIS (to prevent fraud in the H-1B petition process). Other agencies such as Immigration and Customs Enforcement (ICE) and Customs and Border Protection (CBP) can also become involved. Of these two types of H-1B investigation, by far the more difficult and potentially dangerous for the employer is the LCA audit by the DOL's Wage and Hour Division.

The Honor System

A Labor Condition Application (LCA) is like a tax return. Both are initially reviewed by the government for formal compliance and then are accepted as true. In the case of a tax return, the tax paid is accepted or the requested refund paid. Similarly, an LCA is presumed to be true and is approved if it is formally compliant, whereupon it may be used as part of the H-1B petition.

However, both a tax return and an LCA are subject to later audits. The benefits previously provided may be revoked, penalties may be assessed, and—in the case of fraud—criminal prosecution may be undertaken. This chapter explains the government's process for investigating LCAs and H-1B petitions, how employers should react to such investigations, and the potential penalties for noncompliance.

These matters should be of concern primarily to employers. Absent collusion or conspiracy, there is no LCA liability for H-1B employees. However, employees may wish to pay some attention to employer compliance, because one of the penalties that may be imposed on employers—back pay—can be a benefit to employees. In addition, any failure of the employer to follow requirements can result in the employee's losing H-1B status and becoming subject to arrest and removal (as discussed in Chapter 10).

How Important Is Compliance with the LCA Rules?

It is impossible to overstate the importance of following the LCA rules for the employer and the employee. There can be draconian penalties for both if the rules are not followed. This chapter focuses on the employer's obligations under the Department of Labor's LCA regulations and on the consequences of an employer's failure to abide by them. In Chapter 10, we discuss the issue of LCA compliance from the point of view of the employee.

Example In 2011, a public school district in Maryland was audited and reached a settlement with the Department of Labor agreeing to: (1) pay back wages to 1,044 H-1B workers in the amount of $4,222,146; (2) pay an additional $100,000 as a civil money penalty because some of the violations were "willful" (that is, the employer knew its actions were wrong or acted in reckless disregard for whether its actions were impermissible); and (3) be barred from filing H-1B petitions or requests for permanent residence for a period of two years. These severe penalties resulted from the school district's actions in requiring H-1B employees to pay the attorney fees and filing fee expenses associated with filing for H-1B visas, against LCA rules.[1]

---

[1] "Prince George's County Public Schools agrees to pay $4.2 million in back wages for violations of H-1B temporary foreign worker program": WHD press release No. 11-0996-NAT, July 7, 2011, www.dol.gov/whd/media/press/whdpressVB3.asp?pressdoc=national/20110707.xml#.UMQaFOTO2MQ

 Example   In 2012, an IT consulting company was audited and ordered to pay back wages in the amount of $983,039.12 and civil money penalties of $405,175. The company was also barred from filing any H-1B petitions for a period of two years.[2]

These are only a couple of the many examples of the serious consequences for employers who are audited and found to have violated the LCA regulations.

Processing of LCA Audits

An LCA audit can arise as a random matter but more often is generated by a complaint to the Department of Labor made either by a disaffected former employee or by a US worker who resents the company's employment of foreign workers. Once the matter is in the hands of the Department of Labor for processing, it goes to the Wage and Hour Division, which also has responsibility for compliance with overtime and minimum wage statutes. This is one of the more formidable government agencies and is justifiably feared by US employers.

The audit typically starts with a letter from the Wage and Hour Division informing the company that it has been scheduled for a review to determine its compliance with the LCA regulations. A WHD letter from 2011 is reproduced in Appendix 9-1. Among the items it asks the employer to provide are the following:

- Payroll records for all current and former employees employed for a one-year period

- Corresponding time records for those employees

- All the LCAs submitted during this time period

- Documentation of the wage rate to be paid to each of the H-1B workers

- A full and clear explanation of the system used to set the Actual Wage the company paid for all occupations in which it employed H-1B workers during this time period

- Copies of the LCA notices that were posted

---

[2] "US Labor Department obtains nearly $1 million in back wages and interest for 135 H-1B workers of Smartsoft International": WHD Press Release No. 10-1111-ATL (483), August 17, 2010, www.dol.gov/whd/media/press/whdpressVB2print.asp?pressdoc=Southeast/20100817.xml

- The names, job titles, and contact information (addresses, phone numbers, emails) of all H-1B workers employed during the period and a great deal of specific detail with respect to each of them

- The names, job titles, phone numbers, and addresses of all US workers employed in the same capacity as the H-1B workers during that time period

- The public access files for all the H-1B employees

The WHD letter gives the employer 72 hours to produce the requested documents.

⇨ **Tip** If your company receives such an audit letter, you should immediately contact your immigration attorney. The attorney may be able to negotiate some additional time to gather the requested documents.

The possible violations that DOL can investigate are extensive. The Wage and Hour Administrator will investigate and determine whether an H-1B employer has violated LCA regulations by any of the following acts of omission or commission:

- Filed an LCA which misrepresents a material fact. (Federal criminal statutes provide penalties of up to $10,000 and up to five years in jail for making false statements to the US government.)

- Failed to pay wages as required (including benefits provided as compensation for services and payment of wages for nonproductive time).

- Failed to provide the required working conditions.

- Filed an LCA during a strike or lockout in the occupational classification at the place of employment.

- Failed to provide notices of the filing of the LCA.

- Failed to specify accurately on the LCA the number of workers sought, the occupational classification in which the H-1B employee will be employed, or the wage rate and conditions of employment.

- Failed to comply with the additional requirements of a *dependent employer.*

- Required or accepted from an H-1B employee payment of the $750 or $1,500 training fee.

- Required or attempted to require an H-1B nonimmigrant to pay a penalty for ceasing employment prior to an agreed upon date.

- Discriminated against an employee for whistleblower activities.

- Failed to make available for public examination the application and necessary document(s) at the employer's principal place of business or worksite.

- Failed to maintain required documentation.

- Failed otherwise to comply with the LCA requirements.

The Penalties for LCA Violations

Civil penalties for LCA violations can include back wages, the value of benefits that should have been paid, and civil monetary fines. Back wages and benefits are equal to the difference between the salary and benefits the employer paid to the H-1B employee and the amount it should have paid under the LCA. Penalties for LCA violations can amount to tens of thousands of dollars for a single employee and millions of dollars for employers with a large H-1B workforce.

Civil monetary fines fall into three categories, with the maximum amount of the fine within each category depending on the nature of the violation as follows:

- A maximum fine of $1,000 per violation for:

  - A violation pertaining to a strike or lockout

  - A substantial violation pertaining to LCA notices or LCA specificity

  - A negligent misrepresentation of material fact on the LCA

  - An early-termination penalty paid by the employee

  - Payment by the employee of the $750 or $1,500 Training Fee

- A maximum fine of $5,000 per violation for:

  - An intentional failure pertaining to wages or working conditions, a strike or lockout, LCA notices, or LCA specificity

  - An intentional misrepresentation of a material fact on the LCA.

- A maximum fine of $35,000 per violation where an employer displaced a U.S. worker in conjunction with:

  - A willful violation of rules pertaining to wages or working condition, strike or lockout, LCA notices, LCA specificity; or

  - A willful misrepresentation of a material fact on the labor condition application

Within a given category, the DOL enjoys wide statutory discretion in determining the amount of a civil monetary fine in consideration of the following factors:

- Employer's previous history of violations

- The number of workers affected by the violation or violations

- The gravity of the violation or violations

- Efforts made by the employer in good faith to comply

- The employer's explanation of the violation or violations

- The employer's commitment to future compliance

- The extent to which the employer achieved a financial gain due to the violation, and the potential financial or other loss with respect to other parties

Debarment—the disqualification or suspension of an employer's eligibility to obtain DOL approval of H-1B LCAs or employment-based green card petitions—may accompany these civil money penalties. The periods of debarment depend on the category of civil monetary fines: at least one year for the $1,000 violations, two years for the $5,000 violations, and three years for the $35,000 violations. Criminal penalties for both the company and its officers are possible in extreme cases of fraud. Charges brought against employers have included conspiracy, mail fraud, wire fraud, and making false statements in an immigration matter.

Procedurally, a negotiated settlement can be reached between the Wage and Hour Division and the employer, as was the case in the Maryland school district example given above; or the Wage and Hour Administrator may issue a determination, as in the IT Consulting Company example given above. The Administrator's determination can be challenged by the employer before an Administrative Law Judge and that decision can be appealed by either party to the Administrative Review Board. Court review in the federal District Court is also theoretically possible, but no employer has yet deemed it worthwhile to seek such review.

 # USCIS Site Visits to Detect Fraud

In 2004, USCIS established the Fraud Detection and National Security (FDNS) unit to deter fraud and protect national security. Every new H-1B petition must be accompanied by a $500 fee designated for fraud prevention. As a result, the activities of the FDNS unit are very well funded, and the number of such site visits is increasing. An employer should be prepared in case there is such a visit. Initially, the visits were carried out by private firms contracted by FDNS; now they tend to be conducted by USCIS agents.

In contrast to the DOL audits of LCAs, the H-1B site visits normally are limited to verifying the facts concerning one randomly selected I-129 petition. Even if the employer has filed many H-1B petitions, the site visits so far focus only on the one petition. Basically the agent wants to verify that there is a real employer, a real job, and that the individual is working in the job indicated on the I-129 petition at the location and at the salary shown on the petition.

Unlike DOL audits, which are initiated by a letter, USCIS site visits are unannounced. The agent typically arrives at the business premises and asks to speak to the person who signed the I-129 petition. If that person is unavailable, he will ask to speak to another employer representative, such as someone in HR. USCIS regulations allow the government to investigate the facts concerning the I-129 petition.[3] Moreover, the I-129 petition signed by the employer expressly states: "The Petitioner acknowledges the legal authority to audit and verify all benefit eligibility data by means determined appropriate by USCIS including the conduct of random on-site inspections." Therefore, USCIS takes the position that it does not need a subpoena.

---

[3] 8 CFR 103, 204-205, 214.

💣 **Caution**   It may be advisable to establish a policy not to admit any unauthorized person to the private areas of the business without the approval of HR or your attorney. Voluntarily admitting an agent to such areas would waive any possible Fourth Amendment claims. The agent's business card should be obtained to confirm identity, and you may want to ask to have the attorney who has filed an appearance form on the case (Form G-28) participate by telephone.

The agent will ask for specific information about the company, its business, and the number of employees. She may ask to see company documents, including tax returns. She will ask the company representative about the job title, job duties, work location, and salary, and she will ask for copies of recent pay stubs and W-2 forms. After getting the company representative's answers to these questions, the agent will ask to speak personally with the employee to ask him the same questions.

Once the site visit and any follow-up are completed, the agent decides whether there is a need to conduct further inquiry. If the agent cannot verify the facts on the I-129, or if there are significant discrepancies, a denial or revocation proceeding may be initiated. If the agent determines there is fraud (such as no work site), the matter may be referred to ICE for criminal investigation. Revocation proceedings and ICE criminal investigations happen very rarely.

Types of issues that FDNS identifies in its H-1B program investigations (in a very small percentage of cases) include the following:

- The petitioner's business does not physically exist.

- The petitioner misrepresented the details of the beneficiary's employment.

- The beneficiary is not or will not be employed at the listed location or area.

- The beneficiary is not or will not be performing the duties specified on the petition.

- The petitioner withdrew the petition.

- The petitioner is not paying the beneficiary the certified wage.

📑 **Takeaway**   For most legitimate employers there is no reason to fear USCIS site visits, provided that the employee is working in the job and at the location listed on the I-129 and is being paid the salary shown on the form.

Maintaining H-1B Status

Both employer and employee have a strong interest in maintaining the employee in legal H-1B status. But the employee and his family have more on the line personally. The H-1B employee has made a major life decision in deciding to leave his home country to work and live in the US. The consequences to the worker and his family of falling out of legal status can be severe and sometimes catastrophic on a personal level. For that reason, we urge all H-1B workers to take a personal interest in maintaining their legal status and not simply rely on the employer or the employer's attorney to take care of everything.

Make Sure You Are Familiar with the Details

The employer will provide you with a copy of the H-1B application, including the Labor Condition Application (LCA). You need to be familiar with what it says about where you will be working, your job title, the description of your job duties, and your salary. You must be able to answer these questions both at the consulate when applying for a visa stamp, at the airport when arriving in the US, and—once in the US—to verify the legitimacy of the H-1B to officials of DOL or USCIS. Failure to correctly answer these questions can lead to delayed or denied visas, denial of admission to the US, and even arrest and removal from the US in extreme cases.

Paying Attention to Expiration Dates

It is clear that both employer and employee should be paying close attention to the expiration date of the H-1B to ensure that an extension is filed before that date. As long as the extension application is filed before the date the H-1B status expires, as shown on the Form I-94, the H-1B employee is considered to be in legal status for at least 240 days until the extension application has been acted upon. Note that the extension cannot be filed more than six months before the expiration of the current H-1B. Various other complications often arise in unexpected ways with respect to both the H-1B worker and the worker's family members in H-4 status.

The Expiring Passport Trap

Typically, the initial H-1B petition will be approved for three years and the initial visa stamp issued for a three-year period. An exception to this is visa reciprocity rules requiring that the visa be issued for a shorter period because the person's home country similarly limits visas for US citizens.

Admission for a shorter period than that on the approved petition and the visa stamp is a trap that has ensnared many. The officer at the airport will often (although not always) limit the admission period on the Form I-94 to the date of expiration of the individual's passport, regardless of the validity date shown on the H-1B approval notice. If the employee fails to notice the discrepancy or to bring it to the attention of the company or its lawyers, the consequences can be grim. The H-1B employee falls out of status on the date of expiration of the I-94 (even though the visa and H-1B petition are still date-valid) and begins to accrue "unlawful status" in the US. Once out of status, it is not possible to extend one's stay in the US without departing and making a new entry (although USCIS may forgive the late filing if there are compelling reasons for having failed to file on time). If the period of "unlawful presence" (in this example, staying after the I-94 expiration date) exceeds 180 days, upon departing the US the individual will be barred from returning for 3 years; if the period exceeds one year, the individual will be barred for 10 years.

If this situation occurs—that the visa stamp and petition are still date-valid but the I-94 issued at the airport is limited to an earlier date—it is essential for the employee to inform the company and attorney this has happened and extend the passport validity at the first opportunity. Once the passport has been extended, and before the expiration date on the I-94, the employer must file an application to extend the worker's stay in the US with USCIS on Form I-129. (In this case, the employer is filing to "extend" the worker's stay to the original petition approval date and beyond the expiration of the I-94.)

This does not require a new LCA unless the employer is seeking an extension beyond the original petition approval date. It requires only the basic filing fee, not the additional training fee.

⚖ Failure to Extend Family Members' H-4 Status

An unfortunate misconception held by some H-1B workers is that it is not necessary to also extend the H-4 status of their spouse or children when they extend their own H-1B status. Apparently they think that their family's status is automatically extended when they extend their H-1B status. This misunderstanding may originate at the time of the original issuance of the H-1B and H-4 visas. No separate petition approval is required for the H-4 dependents' initial visa-stamping: they tag along based on the H-1B petition approval and proof of their relationship to the H-1B worker. However, status in the US is limited to the period of authorized stay (currently on Form I-94, although this document will be phased out). If the date of authorized stay expires without the H-1B worker's having filed an H-4 extension application (on Form I-539), the spouse or child falls out of status and begins accruing "unlawful presence" (and potentially faces a 3- to 10-year bar from returning to the US).

Different considerations apply for H-4 family member extensions when the worker is moving to a new employer that is seeking an extension of the period of the H-1B petition in addition to approval of the change of employer. If an H-4 dependent's I-94 has a significant period of continuing validity, there may be no need to extend the H-4 along with the H-1B. The validity of the H-4 status is not dependent on the H-1B employee's working for any particular employer, so when she changes employers, the H-4 spouse or child is not required to do anything as long as the date on the I-94 is still valid.

This is particularly true if it is known that the H-4 spouse or child intends to travel outside the US before the expiration date of the current H-4 visa and I-94. In that case, the H-4 dependent would be admitted for the period shown on the new employer's H-1B approval notice for the H-1B worker. Nothing would be gained by filing an I-539 extending the I-94 before this trip. On the other hand, if no travel is contemplated in the near future, it may be wise to keep the validity date of the H-4 dependent the same as that of the H-1B employee to avoid the risk of overlooking the H-4 expiration date. This is especially true if the I-94 expiration date for the H-4 dependent will be earlier than that of the H-1B employee after the extension has been approved.

The problem of losing H-4 status often comes to light in one of two very unfortunate ways. One is when the affected H-4 spouse or child departs the US and seeks a new visa to return. At that point, he may learn for the first time that failure to extend the H-4 status in the US has created a bar to returning. The other is when an H-4 dependent applies for permanent resident (green card) status. Applications for adjustment of status to permanent residence for employment-based immigrants and their families require that none of these individuals has been out of status or worked without authorization for more than 180 days. If the legal stay of the H-4 spouse or child was not extended when the H-1B was extended, and if that was not discovered within 180 days after the H-4 expiration date shown on the I-94, then that H-4 dependent cannot adjust his or her status to permanent resident in the US. Moreover, when that H-4 spouse or child departs the US to go for an immigrant visa interview at a consulate, he or she will be barred from returning to the US for at least three years (ten years if the overstay exceeded one year).

Takeaway   It is critically important for you to make sure that your family members' H-4 status is extended when your H-1B status is extended.

Changing H-1B Employers

If you are employed in the US in valid H-1B status, you can begin working for a new H-1B employer as soon as that employer has properly filed a nonfrivolous petition (this continuing employment authorization is referred to as **porting**). If the new employer's petition for you were ultimately denied, however, you would at that time be out of status. Some people are comfortable making the move to new employment as soon as USCIS has received the application; others move only after the fee receipt has been issued; and still others move only after the new petition has been approved. For most people most of the time, starting work for the new employer once there is confirmation of delivery of the application works out fine. Occasionally, the application may be returned because of an unsigned filing fee check or one in the wrong amount. Very, very rarely, a petition may be denied.

Caution   You need to exercise some caution when making the move to new H-1B employment. For example, it may be risky for you to give notice to your current employer that you are leaving before the new employer has filed its petition for you. Should the employer decide to terminate you immediately, you would be out of status as of the date the employer sends a letter to USCIS notifying them of your termination. If that date is earlier than the date USCIS receives the new employer's petition for you, the request to extend your H-1B status may be denied, on the grounds that you were out of status, even if the new employer's H-1B petition has been approved. The net effect would be that upon notification of this action by USCIS, you would have to stop working for the new employer until you depart the US and make a new entry, showing the H-1B approval notice for the new employer.

 # Vulnerability for Certain LCA Violations

There are some very strong arguments that the individual H-1B worker's legal status should not be negatively affected by an employer's violations of the Labor Condition Application rules. The statutory provisions clearly give DOL responsibility for regulating and enforcing the LCA provisions, for which employers are accountable, and give USCIS responsibility for the provisions relating specifically to the H-1B petition and the individual's legal status in the US. Nevertheless, as a practical matter it is clear that employer violations have brought grief to individual H-1B workers with respect to at least one LCA issue—the location of the employment.

⇨ **Example**   In January 2000, immigration agents arrested forty Indian IT workers at an Air Force base in San Antonio, Texas. Their companies had filed H-1B petitions and LCAs authorizing their employment in Houston, not San Antonio.[1]

⇨ **Example**   In January 2010, a number of H-1B IT workers were denied entry at Newark and JFK airports. They were singled out, questioned, and issued expedited removal orders (which carry a 5-year bar from returning to the US!) because they were arriving to work at a client site or third-party site other than the location shown on the employer's LCA and H-1B petition. These actions were triggered by an overzealous interpretation of a memo issued earlier that month by Donald Neufeld, Associate Director of Service Center Operations for USCIS.

While these instances involved alleged violations of the LCA regulations, they also were considered by the USCIS and CBP to violate provisions of the regulations governing H-1B petitions and the requirements surrounding the employer/employee relationship.

---

[1] www.indolink.com/NRINews/Community/arrestH1.html

⚒ ✸ Caution The USCIS and CBP consider that without a valid LCA the H-1B petition is not valid, making the H-1B worker subject to deportation or denial of entry into the US.

Permissible Side Activities

The H-1B worker must be careful not to invalidate his or her H-1B status by engaging in any prohibited side activities. Certain activities are clearly permissible, such as studying or passive investing. Concurrent employment is allowed if the requirements below are met.

Additional Employment

As long as a concurrent H-1B petition is approved first, the H-1B worker can have a second job. Part-time employment is completely fine as long as both the Labor Condition Application and I-129 petition clearly identify the employment as part-time. If full-time employment changes to part-time employment, it is necessary for the employer to file a new Labor Condition Application and amended I-129 petition before the worker moves from full-time to part–time hours. It is not necessary to wait for approval of the amended petition before making the change in hours; it can be done upon filing of the petition.

✸ Caution Self-employment is not allowed.

⚒ Starting a Company

Many H-1B workers ask whether they may start their own company while in H-1B status. They are allowed to do so as long as starting the company does not involve actively working for the company. Although the line between organizing and establishing a new company and performing productive work for that company can be somewhat blurred, we are not aware of any government interest in limiting activities in this area. Once the company is established and operating, the H-1B worker may take a position with the newly established company as soon as the company has filed either a transfer or concurrent H-1B petition on her behalf. Again, it is important to understand that self-employment is not allowed under the H-1B rules, which require a separate employer and employee.

International Travel

Under certain circumstances, international travel can jeopardize an H-1B worker's status. We previously discussed the dangers of departing the United States after inadvertently overstaying the I-94 authorized time by more than 180 days. What about traveling outside the US while an extension or change of status application has been filed but has not yet been decided?

Travel While an H-1B Extension Is Pending

Leaving the US while an extension of H-1B petition has been filed but not yet approved will not invalidate or cancel the extension petition. There is no difficulty if the H-1B worker departs after the extension petition has been filed and returns to the US before his old H-1B visa expires. But if the old visa has expired, he will not be able to return to the US until the extension petition has been approved and he has obtained a new visa stamp.

Travel with Change of Employer Petition Pending

An H-1B worker is allowed to use a prior employer's H-1B visa if it has not expired, so she can travel outside the US while an application for a change of H-1B employer is pending. By showing the I-797 receipt notice indicating that the change of employer petition was filed in a timely fashion, she is legally entitled to enter the US before the new petition has been approved. This policy was reaffirmed in a July 12, 2012, meeting between the American Immigration Lawyers Association (AILA) and Customs and Border Protection (CBP), as follows:

> *When the nonimmigrant alien presents the valid H-1B visa based upon an approved petition from Employer A and a Form I-797 Notice of Receipt for the pending petition filed by Employer B (the new employer for whom the alien now works based upon H-1B portability), the alien should be admitted through the visa validity date. If, because of visa reciprocity, the visa validity is shorter than the petition validity stated on the visa, the admission should be through the petition validity date.*

⇨ Tip   If you plan to enter the US with your unexpired H-1B visa from a previous employer and a receipt notice (I-797) for the H-1B petition of a new employer, you should take with you a copy of the 2001 memo in case the CBP officer at the airport or border is not fully versed in these portability rules. Another option would be to use Premium Processing to obtain approval of the new H-1B petition before returning from abroad.

If the prior visa stamp has already expired, the returning worker would first have to get a new H-1B visa at the US embassy or consulate before returning to the US.

🏃 Travel with Change of Status Application Pending

The prospective H-1B employer's petition may request a change of status from another non-immigrant status such as visitor or student. In that situation, it is clear that departing the US before the petition has been approved will cancel the request for change of status. If the H-1B petition is ultimately approved, you must obtain an H-1B visa and return to the US before obtaining legal H-1B status, as it would not happen via the earlier change of status application. In the alternative, a new change of status application could be filed after the individual has returned to the US (for example, in F-1 student status) and after the underlying H-1B petition has been approved.

🏃 The Last Action Rule

When a person travels abroad while an application for extension of stay is pending, or after a change of status has been approved but before its effective date, the question can arise whether the I-94 issued upon the return to the US or the I-94 on the approved Form I-797 is the controlling document. In a 2004 exchange of letters, Efren Hernandez of the USCIS Office of Adjudications stated that the "last action" is when the I-797 takes effect. That particular situation involved an application for change of status from F-1 to H-1B, approved in August 2004 but not effective until December 1, 2004. The individual both traveled abroad and returned to the US in September 2004. The change of status took effect on December 1, 2004, and superseded the I-94 issued to the person in September. Keep in mind that policy letters such as that one are not binding on USCIS, and the policy could change in the future. In the case of travel after filing an application for extension of stay (either with the existing employer or a new employer), and return before the application has been approved, the Form I-797 approving the extension of stay governs.

🏃 Travel after Company Ownership or Name Changes

In the section "Issues for Employers" below, we discuss what is required of the employer when there have been changes in the company's name or ownership, such as a merger or acquisition. In many of these situations, there is no requirement that the employer file any new petition for the H-1B worker until an extension application must be filed.

However, from the H-1B worker's point of view, it may be desirable for the employer to submit an amended petition so that there will be an approval notice with the correct company name to show to CBP when the worker reenters the US. If a new visa stamp is needed for some reason, such as reciprocity rules causing a shorter-term prior visa than I-797 approval time, getting the new visa stamped without a petition approval in the new employer name may be difficult, since the consular officer is unlikely to be aware of the corporate restructuring rules. Likewise, the CBP officer may not understand the rules and may cause delays and other problems on the employee's arrival in the US.

Change of Address Notification

With very few exceptions, all non-US citizens are required by law to notify USCIS of their change of address within 10 days of moving their residence. They are required to file **Form AR-11**,[2] either by mail or online at egov.uscis. gov/crisgwi/go?action=coa.Terms.

They are also advised to change the address on any pending or recently approved applications or petitions, either online or by telephone at 1-800-375-5283. It is most convenient to use the online change of address system to complete both requirements at the same time. Once Form AR-11 is completed online, the opportunity is provided on the same website to change the address on any pending or recently approved applications by entering the case file numbers. That will help ensure that future notices from USCIS will go to the correct address.

Issues for Employers

The matters discussed in the sections above also pertain to employers. To avoid the severe penalties discussed in Chapter 9 for violating the LCA rules, employers must ensure that their H-1B workers remain in valid status. They must pay attention to expiration dates, follow the employer "porting" rules, and carefully monitor and support the international travel of these employees. Other issues of maintaining status are primarily employer-related.

---

[2] www.uscis.gov/files/form/ar-11.pdf

🐾 Changes in the Employing Entity

There are times when an H-1B employer changes its name or undergoes a structural change through a merger, acquisition, or other corporate restructuring. In these circumstances, the employer must do what is required to keep its H-1B workers in legal status. Those actions will vary depending on the specific details of the changes.

It is now clear that the employer is not required to file a new LCA or I-129 petition just because it changes its name or has a change in ownership, provided everything else about the employment remains the same. If there is an ownership change, even one involving a new taxpayer ID number, DOL regulations now allow the new entity to adopt the H-1B employees by assuming the LCA obligations of the predecessor entity without the filing of a new LCA. The new entity is required, however, to keep a list of the transferred H-1B nonimmigrants and to maintain in its public access files a document containing the following:

- A list of each LCA by number and date of certification

- A description of the new employing entity's actual wage system applicable to the workers

- The Federal Tax ID Number (FEIN) of the new employing entity

- A sworn statement by an authorized representative of the new employing entity, acknowledging its assumption of the obligations specified in the LCAs filed by its predecessor and agreeing to abide by the DOL regulations applicable to LCAs, to keep a copy of the sworn statement in the public access files, and to make it available upon request to the public or any representative of DOL

Normally the immigration attorney will assist in preparing this documentation.

Under USCIS rules, an amended H-1B petition is not required in circumstances where the new entity succeeds to the interests and obligations of the original petitioning employer, and the terms and conditions of employment otherwise remain the same.

For any new H-1B hires or when it seeks an extension for any of the existing H-1B workers, the new entity is required to file a new LCA and H-1B petition in its own name. Also, when an H-1B worker is contemplating international travel, it may be worthwhile for the new entity to file a new H-1B petition, even if not legally required to do so, in order to make the international travel easier for the employee.

❧ Changes in the Location of the Job

If the H-1B employee is moved to a new work location with no other material change in the terms and conditions of employment, is it necessary to file a new LCA or a new or amended H-1B petition? That depends.

If the new work-site address is within the same "area of intended employment," usually defined as the normal commuting distance, DOL does not require the filing of a new LCA. But it does require that the original LCA notice be posted in two places at the new location before the H-1B worker begins working there (see Chapter 8). If the new location is outside the area of intended employment and will be for more than 30 days in a year, a new LCA is required.

The USCIS rules for when an amended H-1B petition is required are not as clear. In October 2003, USCIS issued a letter (reproduced in Appendix 10-1), confirming that an amended H-1B petition would not be required simply based on a move to another location. As long as an LCA for the new location was approved after proper work-site posting before the employee worked at the new site, no amended petition would be required. This position is currently being reevaluated by USCIS as a part of its overall policy review. More significantly, the California Service Center is taking the position that an amended H-1B petition should be filed whenever a new LCA is filed. To be safe, that would be the best course for employers to follow.

Extending the 6-Year Limit on H-1Bs

H-1B status is normally limited to a total of six years (and time in L-1 status is counted in those six years). However, it is possible for that six-year limit to be extended indefinitely if an application for permanent residence has been started in time.

That was made possible by the American Competitiveness in the Twenty-First Century Act (AC21), which provides for an H-1B extension until the H-1B worker becomes a permanent resident, as long as a *Labor Certification Application* or immigrant visa petition on Form I-140 is filed at least one year before the legal H-1B period expires. Normally that means that the Labor Certification Application or Form I-140 must be filed before the end of the employee's fifth year in H-1B status. Since it may take several months to complete recruitment before filing a Labor Certification Application, such cases should be started before the H-1B employee completes four and a half years in H-1B status, in order to make sure that the application can be filed before the end of the fifth year. As long as the Labor Certification Application or Form I-140 is pending or approved, the H-1B status can be extended beyond six years in one-year increments. Even if it were initially denied, the Labor Certification Application or Form I-140 is considered to be pending if an administrative appeal from the denial is pending.

⇨ **Terminology Note**   The *Labor Certification Application*, the first step in obtaining permanent resident status, should not be confused with the *Labor Condition Application* required in the H-1B process, even though both can have the same acronym ("LCA"). Normally, "LCA" refers to the H-1B Labor Condition Application only.

AC21 provides for an even longer extension of three years if a Form I-140 petition has been *approved* (not just filed) for the H-1B worker (by any employer, not just the current H-1B employer) and if the immigration quota prevents the worker from applying for a green card. Whether the immigration quota prevents an immediate application for a green card can be determined by comparing the "priority date"—the date the Labor Certification Application or I-140 petition was filed—with the "cutoff date." The "cutoff date" can be found in the monthly Visa Bulletin issued by the State Department, at travel. state.gov/visa/bulletin/bulletin_1360.html.

Tip   Leveraging AC21, workers from certain oversubscribed countries like India and China—especially those whose jobs do not require five years of experience or a master's degree—often can work in H-1B status for 10 or 15 years before their green cards are finally available.

In order to meet the requirement of filing the first step of the green card process while a year of H-1B status remains, it is sometimes necessary for the H-1B worker to "recapture" time he has spent outside the United States during his period of H-1B employment. For example, an H-1B teacher who spends three months every summer outside the US may have more than a year of time he needs to recapture. It may be necessary to do that in order to have the H-1B period continue for more than one year after the green card case (Labor Certification Application or Form I-140) is filed. In some cases, an employer may need to send the H-1B worker abroad for a period of time to make sure that a full year of H-1B eligibility is remaining when the Labor Certification Application is filed.

Likewise, an employer may need to use Premium Processing to expedite the processing of the I-140 petition in order to make the H-1B worker eligible for the 3-year extension of H-1B status.

Takeaway   As long as either the Labor Certification Application is filed while one year of H-1B eligibility remains, or an I-140 petition is approved before the worker files the application for extension, the H-1B worker's stay can be extended beyond the 6-year limit.

Termination of H-1B Employment

No job lasts forever. There are many reasons why employees may leave their H-1B employment, and many reasons why they may be forced to leave.

 ## Strategies for H-1B Employees

A common reason for an H-1B employee to leave a job is that the employer has not provided a credible pathway to permanent residence. After several years of working in the US and enjoying the benefits of life in the US, most H-1B employees wish to stay. If the employer is not willing to sponsor a labor certification application or other green card solution, H-1B employees should consider changing to an employer that will.

Normally, green card sponsorship will not be part of the negotiations for initial H-1B employment. For one thing, the employee does not have much bargaining power at that point. However, green card sponsorship could be discussed after you have worked for the H-1B employer for a while (and proved yourself to be a valuable employee), and it should also be discussed when you seek a new H-1B employer.

Another reason H-1B employees leave their employment is one that often motivates US employees to leave their jobs: they believe they should be paid more. Unlike other employees, H-1B employees have the recourse of demanding back wages through the Labor Condition Application (LCA) enforcement procedures discussed in Chapter 9. Although the LCA regulations provide for protection against retaliation when an employee makes an LCA complaint, as a practical matter it is best to make such complaints only after the employment has ended. Even if the employer complies with the anti-retaliation rules, remaining in the job after you have made a complaint could create a very uncomfortable work environment. In addition, an employer can refuse to sponsor a green card, and since the H-1B employment is temporary, that refusal alone would compel the H-1B employee to leave eventually in any event.

Employers, of course, may have many reasons for terminating employees, even if they are pleased with the employee's performance. Competitive pressures may force employers to reduce staff or change the focus of their businesses. They may wish to hire different workers with different skills. Generally, it is a good idea not to take termination personally and to understand that employers often need to lay off employees in order to remain profitable.

Find Another Job Soon

Although in private you may throw your shoe against the wall and curse your boss when you get notice of the impending termination, it is important that you make an extra effort in public to be professional and understanding. You have more to lose than most employees do: not just your job, but potentially your home, your car, and your life in America. This is the worst time to become overtly emotional, at least with your employer.

Instead, you should immediately negotiate with your employer to extend your employment for the longest time possible. That will give you the opportunity to find a new job and, once you find a job, more time to file a new H-1B petition.

One way to extend your employment is to use accrued vacation or paid time off (PTO) time. Instead of cashing out those accrued benefits, you may be able to persuade the employer to keep you on the payroll and terminate your employment after you have used up your vacation time. To preserve that possibility, it is a good idea to save your vacation time. If you have three weeks of vacation time saved, that is an additional three weeks to look for another job.

⇨ **Note** The employer cannot simply keep you on the payroll as an employee and not pay you, as a means to afford you more time to find a job. That would violate the *benching* rule, discussed in Chapter 8.

The official policy of USCIS is that your H-1B status ends the moment the underlying employment ends. This policy was first confirmed in a letter dated March 27, 2001, from a senior official of the Immigration and Naturalization Service (the predecessor of USCIS). That letter confirms that H-1B status ends "immediately upon termination" and that the H-1B employee must quickly depart the United States. On December 9, 2008, in a meeting with representatives from the American Immigration Lawyers Association (AILA), USCIS confirmed this policy as follows:

> If the underlying H-1B petition is already approved, the general rule is that the approval of any petition is automatically revoked if the petitioner goes out of business, as the employer-employee relationship has ended. . . . Once the underlying H-1B petition is revoked, the Beneficiary's H-1B status terminates as of the date the employment ceased, pursuant to <u>Matter of Lee</u>, 11 I. & N. Dec. 601 (Reg. Comm. 1966), or the date the petition was revoked, **whichever is later**. The Beneficiary is in violation of status the day after the employment was terminated.

Although this statement is directed to a situation where an employer goes out of business, it appears to be equally applicable to the end of the employer-employee relationship when the employee quits or is fired.

Despite these dire pronouncements, in the past USCIS has been more flexible—and at one time even proposed a 30-day grace period for changing to other employment. We have found in our law practices that USCIS may approve extension of H-1B status if the new employer files the new H-1B petition within a few weeks of the termination of previous employment. However, its treatment of these "late" filings is erratic, and some USCIS examiners will deny the extension of status when the worker is unemployed for just a few days. For you to prove that you have been working for the original employer—and therefore maintaining your H-1B status—USCIS will require your two most recent paycheck stubs in all cases involving a change of employer.

⚜ Get Back into H-1B Status by Leaving the US

Even if it takes more than 30 days to find a new job and your H-1B status ends, you might still be able to get back into H-1B status quickly after you find a new qualifying job. Although USCIS might not extend your H-1B status, it would probably approve the new H-1B petition if you qualify.

⇨ **Note** Although not very clear and often downright confusing, the H-1B form (Form I-129) has a dual purpose for those already in the US. First, it petitions for H-1B approval, to use as the basis for an application for an H-1B visa at a US embassy or consulate abroad. Second, it can seek to extend H-1B status or change to H-1B status from another nonimmigrant status such as student status. Normally those in the US use it for both purposes, but you can use it for one purpose or the other.

With a new H-1B visa approved by USCIS, you can get back into H-1B status even if USCIS finds that you are out of status because you took too long to find another job and file another petition and are therefore ineligible to extend your status. To get right back into H-1B status, you could travel outside of the US, get a new visa at a US consulate abroad, and then return using the new H-1B visa. With Premium Processing, that process might take just a few weeks. As an alternative to getting a new visa, you could simply travel to the border (Canada or Mexico), leave the US, then turn around and come back the same day! In that case, you would simply use your old, *unexpired* H-1B visa, together with your new H-1B approval notice, to reenter the US.

💣 **Caution** An H-1B employee will be barred from returning to the US if he or she remains in the US for *more than 180 days* after the H-1B status expires. For the purpose of applying this bar, the H-1B status does not expire when the employment ends, but on the termination date on Form I-94 (or any extension of that date on Form I-797).

Requirements for Employers

All of the LCA obligations, including payment of the Required Wage and providing normal company benefits, continue until the employee is properly terminated. Back wages, the value of health insurance and other benefits, and interest on those wages and benefits can be awarded to the employee by the Department of Labor, *even if the employee has found another job and has been earning wages and benefits from the new employer.* The purpose of the award of back wages and benefits is not to compensate the employee but to make sure the employer fulfills its LCA obligations.

This obligation to continue to pay was confirmed in a 2011 administrative appellate decision of the Department of Labor. A decision to award back wages, even if the employer no longer employs the H-1B worker, depends on whether there has been a **bona fide termination** of the employment. Without bona fide termination, the employee is simply considered to be in a nonproductive status (i.e., "benched") and is still entitled to the LCA wages and benefits.

There are four parts to bona fide termination, and all four must be completed by the employer to cut off further LCA liability for wages and benefits:

- Presentation to the terminated employee of a memorandum of termination

- Offer to the terminated employee of payment of return transportation

- Withdrawal of the LCA

- Withdrawal of the H-1B petition.

These four parts are considered in turn below.

⚘ Memorandum Confirming Termination

The first part of bona fide termination is making it clear that the employment has terminated. Often, an employee will simply stop working, perhaps because there is not enough work for her, and may seek other employment. It might not be clear whether the employee will return in the future.

It is of crucial importance for the employer to clarify the employment status of the H-1B employee *whenever the H-1B employee stops working* (except perhaps in the case of a normal vacation, short sick leave, or other PTO). To avoid later uncertainty, especially in LCA enforcement proceedings, it is best to prepare a memorandum that clarifies the circumstances of the employment termination or suspension. The memo does not need to be long—just a few sentences should be fine—but it should clarify the situation, and it should be signed by the employee. If the H-1B employee refuses to sign, you should give it to the H-1B employee anyway, and you should also email it to the employee so you have proof that the message was delivered.

The memorandum should identify which of three possible circumstances applies:

- The H-1B employee was fired

- The H-1B employee quit

- The H-1B employee has asked to take unpaid time off (e.g., for maternity leave)

Whether the employee was fired or quit will have consequences not only for LCA obligations, but also for other matters such as the employer's obligation to contribute to unemployment insurance. Whether the employee has asked to take time off, or has been compelled to do so because there is not enough work available, will determine whether there has been "benching" and whether the H-1B employee should continue to be paid while in a nonproductive status.

✿ Payment of Return Transportation

The second part of bone fide termination involves the employer's payment, or offer of payment, for return transportation to the H-1B employee's home country. This obligation for return transportation also depends on whether the employee quit or was fired. If the employee quits, there is no obligation to pay for return transportation; if the employee is fired or laid off (which amounts to the same thing in this case), payment for return transportation is required.

The offer to pay for return transportation should also be in writing and is normally (but does not have to be) in the same memorandum that confirms the employment termination.

What if the employee has no intention of returning to his or her home country? Most H-1B employees who are terminated from their employment simply find employment with another employer willing to sponsor their H-1B status, and they do not go home. Must you pay the return ticket home in that case?

Unfortunately, there is no clear guidance. The rule itself provides as follows:

> *The employer will be liable for the reasonable costs of return transportation of the alien abroad if the alien is dismissed from employment by the employer before the end of the period of authorized admission.*

Clearly, the safest course is simply to pay the H-1B employee a reasonable amount to purchase a one-way ticket home. However, the purpose of the requirement to pay the transportation costs is to make sure that the H-1B employee has the means to leave the US at the end of the H-1B employment. If the H-1B employment will continue (albeit with another employer), you could argue that the requirement to pay those costs has not been triggered. This argument has particular weight since the rule says, "The employer will be liable"—not "the employer must pay." This could be interpreted to mean that if the employee does not go home, there is no obligation to pay.

You may prefer to offer payment (rather than actually pay), but if the employee asks for payment, it is a good idea to pay him or her, regardless of whether you believe the employee will actually leave the US.

Admonition to Employers and Employees We urge both H-1B employers and H-1B employees to try to act in good faith in your dealings with each other and in applying the various rules that govern H-1B employment throughout the entire process, from initial employment negotiations through termination. Neither party should use the rules to attempt to gain an unfair advantage over the other.

Withdrawal of the LCA

The third requirement for bona fide termination is withdrawal of the LCA. That can be done through the iCERT portal, and usually the immigration attorney will handle it. It is a good idea in any event to inform the immigration attorney about the employment termination, so that the attorney's file can be closed and to make sure that you have properly completed all of the required steps for bona fide termination.

Withdrawal of the H-1B Petition

The final step is withdrawal of the H-1B petition itself. That can be done by writing a letter to USCIS, and the attorney can handle this matter as well. USCIS will send a return letter confirming that the petition has been withdrawn.

All of the documentation proving bona fide termination—the memorandum confirming the end of the employment, the offer of transportation costs, withdrawal of the LCA, and withdrawal of the petition—should be placed in the LCA file in the event of a later audit.

The LCA file must be kept for another year, after which it can be destroyed. However, the evidence of bona fide termination should be kept for an additional five years, in case the employee or the Wage and Hour Division (WHD) later claims that the employment was not properly terminated and that the LCA obligations to continue to pay wages and benefits remained in force.

Employee Penalties for Ending the Employment Early

Generally, the employer cannot impose a penalty if an H-1B employee leaves the employment before an agreed-upon date. Normally, that would be an LCA violation, and reimbursement would be enforced after investigation by the WHD.

Furthermore, it is clear that the employer cannot require reimbursement (or deduction from the final paycheck) for any of the H-1B expenses, especially the Training Fee, if the H-1B employee leaves the employment early.

Some states permit a *liquidated damage*, which is an amount an employee must pay for the damages the employer suffers as a result of the employee's breach of the employment contract. Deducting such liquidated damages from the final paycheck would be acceptable only if it was agreed upon in advance of the employment, and only if the damages were a reasonable approximation of the loss actually suffered by the employer. Also, if the liquidated damages were not proper under state law, they would be an LCA violation enforceable by the WHD. Since there are 50 states, all with different employment laws, employers should not draft any liquidated damage clauses in their employment contracts (or at least not try to enforce them) without first consulting an employment lawyer—and, if they are to be applied to H-1B employees, an immigration lawyer as well.

Chapter Takeaway   It is critical for employers to properly terminate an employee to cut off the obligation to pay the salary required under the LCA. That obligation can otherwise continue for the entire term of the LCA, even if the employee has another job and is drawing another salary.

CHAPTER

12

⌨ 🧑 H-1B Alternatives

There is a variety of reasons why an employer might seek an alternative working visa to the H-1B:

- The H-1B quota is filled (see Chapter 3).

- Either the job or the employee does not qualify for H-1B status (see Chapter 4).

- The salary the employer is willing to offer is too low (see Chapter 6).

- The employee will work at multiple client sites, so complying with LCA requirements would be too burdensome (see Chapter 6).

- Some visa categories (E, J, and L) enable spouses to work (see below).

The first of these reasons for seeking an H-1B alternative—the filling of the H-1B quota—is probably the most common. Suppose, for example, you are an employer who identifies a potential professional employee in late April after the quota has been exhausted for the next fiscal year. You would have to wait an entire year before you could petition for H-1B status, and another year and a half before the H-1B employment could begin (see Chapter 3). In that case, you may be able to get another type of working visa for the employee, and then change to H-1B status at a later date once the quota is again available.

In addition to not being quota-limited, most alternative working visas have another feature that employers find attractive: unlike the H-1B visa, they do not require a Labor Condition Application (LCA). That means that there are no required minimum salary, no filing with the Department of Labor, no required recordkeeping, no LCA liability, and no need to post legal notices at each work site. The exceptions are the E-3 and H-1B1 substitute visas, which do require LCAs, as detailed below.

This book is about the H-1B visa, not the alternatives. This chapter is not intended to give you a complete picture of these alternatives. We intend instead to give you an idea of other possibilities and to provide you a basis for consulting with your immigration attorney if you wish to explore these options further.

L-1 Visas for Intracompany Transferees

The *L-1* visa is available only to multinational companies that have already employed the prospective US employee for at least a year in an office outside the US. Specifically, the employee must have worked as a manager, an executive, or a person with company-specific knowledge ("specialized knowledge") for at least one year within the three years preceding the L-1 petition.

The qualifying one year of employment must be spent physically outside the US, and the work must have been done directly for the US employer or for a subsidiary, parent, or affiliate of the US employer. For example, a software developer who has worked for at least a year for the India subsidiary of a US software company might be able to transfer to the parent company in L-1 status.

There are two types of L-1 visas:

- *L-1A visas* are for those who will work in the US as managers or executives.

- *L-1B visas* are for those with **specialized knowledge** of the company's products, services or procedures.

A **manager** usually supervises other employees, but it may be possible to qualify as a "manager" by managing an important company function. For example, the CFO of a small corporation might not supervise any other accountants, but probably would still qualify as a manger if she were solely responsible for the company's accounting functions. The ability to hire and fire other employees (or to help make those types of personnel decisions) is usually an important factor in determining L-1A eligibility. If L-1A eligibility is based primarily on the supervision of other employees, those other employees must be either

- **professional** employees (normally those with college degrees), or
- **managers** who in turn supervise others.

US Citizenship and Immigration Services (USCIS) often takes a restrictive view as to whether an employee possesses company-specific "specialized knowledge" that would justify issuing an L-1B visa. Generally, to qualify in this category, the employee must have worked for the company for several years (not just the minimum one-year eligibility period) and must have essential knowledge that is not generally held throughout the company.

Like the H-1B visa, the L-1 visa begins with a petition to USCIS. Once the petition is approved, the employee will present the petition approval to a US consulate or embassy abroad and obtain the L-1 visa (a stamp in the passport that will be used to gain entry into the US).

Large companies can submit one **blanket L-1 petition** (to establish the requisite corporate relationship between the US **receiving company** and the foreign **sending company**). Once the blanket L-1 petition is approved, an individual petition filed with USCIS is no longer required for each employee. Instead, employees can apply for the L-1 visa directly to the US embassy or consulate, with documents that prove their eligibility as a manager or a person with "specialized knowledge." However, if the consular officer determines that the visa application is "not clearly approvable," an individual petition must be submitted to USCIS. A blanket petition is initially approved for three years and can then be extended indefinitely.

Sometimes It Is Faster to Get a Green Card Than an H-1B Visa!

Rather than wait a year and a half for an H-1B visa, employers may wish to explore **permanent residence (green card)** status. In such cases, the company may be able to start the employee working in the US in half the time it would take to secure H-1B status.

For example, an **Outstanding Researcher** petition can be processed by USCIS in two weeks. Once approved, it may take another 3 to 4 months for the immigrant visa to be issued and for the employee to begin employment in the US.

An "Outstanding Researcher" green card is not limited to those who work for universities or think tanks. A private company may also have a research and development department, and, as long as it employs at least three full-time researchers, it can sponsor the green card. Normally, employees in this category have PhD degrees, but occasionally USCIS will grant a petition to someone who does not.

Others who are eligible for **employment-based green cards** include:

- employees whose work will be in the US **National Interest**

- employees with **Extraordinary Ability** (those who are at the very top of their field)

- **Outstanding Professors**

Like the "Outstanding Researcher" petition, the "Extraordinary Ability" and "Outstanding Professor" petitions can be processed by USCIS in two weeks (using "Premium Processing"). Premium Processing is not available for the "National Interest" petitions, and USCIS will often take 6 months to a year to process those. However, if the potential employee is in the US in another nonimmigrant (temporary) category, such as visitor or student, the "National Interest" petition can be filed with a green card application ("application for adjustment of status"), and USCIS will normally issue an **EAD** (Employment Authorization Document) work card within 90 days.

Another option is a **labor certification**, which is a determination that there is a shortage of US workers who are qualified to do the offered job.[1] Often the labor certification can be completed in 4 to 5 months, and the entire green card case might take less than a year.

💣 ☞ **Caution** Because of quota limitations for employment-based green cards, the labor certification does not work as an H-1B alternative for those born in India or China. It also is not a good H-1B alternative for jobs that do not require at least a bachelor's degree and five years of experience (or a master's degree). Those green card cases can take up to eight years!

However, for highly skilled and experienced professionals born in countries other than India and China, a green card application based on labor certification may be faster than waiting for the H-1B quota to reopen.

---

[1] You can find more information about labor certifications in articles at www.immilaw.com/Newsletters/2005%20January.htm and www.immilaw.com/Newsletters/2009%20Labor%20Cert%20Article.htm.

⇨ **Marriage Benefit Tip 1**   Occasionally, a potential employee has a fiancé or fiancée who is a US citizen. If that potential employee is in the US, even if out of status, an EAD can be obtained within 90 days after marriage.

⇨ **Marriage Benefit Tip 2**   The quota for permanent resident (green card) status depends on country of birth, not country of citizenship. However, a green card applicant can apply within the quota of his or her spouse, if that is more favorable. For example, an EB-2 employment-based green card applicant from India may have to wait more than five years for the quota, but if she were married to someone from Pakistan (it happens!), there would be no quota backlog.

H-1B Substitute Visas for Nationals of Certain Treaty Countries

Treaties with certain trading partners of the US have created visa categories for professionals from those countries that are unavailable to everyone else. For example, the US has a special relationship with Mexico and Canada because they are close neighbors and huge trading partners, and with Australia because of its strategic support for many decades. Chile and Singapore are also important trading partners, and special *H-1B1* visas can be issued to citizens of those countries.

Eligibility for these special visas depends on *citizenship*, not place of birth (the reverse of the dependence of green card eligibility). For example, a person born in China who subsequently becomes an Australian citizen would be eligible for an E-3 visa, described in the next section.

E-3 Visa for Australians

The *E-3* visa is an H-1B substitute that enables professional employment for Australians only, and it should be considered every time the prospective employee is Australian (whether or not an H-1B visa can be obtained immediately). The E-3 visa has the following advantages over the H-1B visa:

- *It is faster.* The application for the E-3 visa is submitted directly to the US consulate, so employer and employee can avoid the weeks or months of waiting required for H-1B petition processing by USCIS.
- *It is cheaper.* The USCIS filing fees (up to $3,550) are avoided.

- *It is not subject to the H-1B quota.* An application can therefore be made at any time during the year, and a lengthy lead time can be avoided.

- *The spouse of an E-3 visa holder can receive authorization to work.*

Eligibility for the E-3 visa is almost identical to that for the H-1B visa, and, as with the H-1B visa, an LCA is required.

✹ ⚖ TN Visas for Canadians and Mexicans

Free Trade Agreements with Canada and Mexico have created a special employment-based visa status for citizens of those countries. It is much like the H-1B visa, in that the **TN** status is for "professionals" and is valid for an initial period of three years.

Like an H-1B case, a TN case can be started with a petition to USCIS, and Premium Processing is available. Alternatively, Canadians may apply for TN status at the border or at an international airport, and they do not require a visa (i.e., a stamp in their passports). Mexicans do require a visa and must apply at the US Embassy in Mexico City or at one of the many US consulates in Mexico.

Unlike H-1B status, which is available for any profession that requires a specialty college degree, TN status is limited to certain professions designated in the treaty.

Spouses of TN employees are granted **TD** status, and, like spouses in H-4 status, they are not allowed to work.

⇨ **Tip**   An LCA is not required for TN status, so TN status is ideal for consultants who will work at multiple client sites.

Canadians can obtain TN status by applying at the border or airport and receiving issuance of a TN document within an hour or so. As an alternative to adjudication at the border, TN petitions may also be submitted to USCIS.

✹ ⚖ H-1B1 for Singaporeans and Chileans

The *H-1B1* visa for Singaporeans and Chileans is subject to a quota, but the quota has never been filled. That means that you can obtain the H-1B1 visa at any time of the year, as soon as you have identified the potential employee. The H-1B1 application is similar to the H-1B petition and requires a preapproved LCA, but the application is submitted directly to the US Embassy in Singapore or Santiago, rather than to USCIS.

💣 **Caution** There are recent reports that the US Embassy in Singapore has been denying H-1B1 visas because it does not believe that certain employees intend to work in the US temporarily. Although State Department guidelines define "temporary" only as a period with "a reasonable, finite end that does not equate to permanent residence," recent denial decisions have insisted upon "strong social and economic ties" to Singapore. Employees applying for an H-1B1 visa should be prepared to demonstrate strong ties to their home country and the probability that they will return there. That is never required for an H-1B visa.

🕯️ 🔨 E-1 and E-2 Visas for European and Other Treaty Countries

E-1 and *E-2* visas are available to owners, managers, and key employees of US companies that are at least 50%-owned by nationals of certain countries with which the US has trade treaties. The US has such treaties with most European countries and Japan, Mexico, and Taiwan.

E-1 visas are for owners, managers, and key employees of US companies that import to or export from the treaty country. To be eligible in this category, at least 50% of the business of the US company must involve trade with the treaty country. For example, a business that imports wine from Italy might be able to obtain E-1 visas for its manager in the US.

💣 **Caution** A key requirement of the E-1 visa is that the trade must be *substantial*—a term that is not very well defined and often depends on the subjective evaluation of the consular officer.

E-2 visas are for the owners, managers, and key employees of US companies that involve a **substantial investment**. Like *substantial trade*, *substantial investment* is not strictly defined, but we have found that a new business that has an initial investment of as little as $150,000 is likely to qualify. The more money invested, the greater the likelihood that the E-2 visa will be granted. Also, a business plan that reflects the potential employment of US workers, as well as a projected growth in revenues and profits, is often required.

In several US embassies, such as Tokyo, London, and Rome, the company can be registered once and determined to be eligible for E-1 and E-2 visas.

Subsequently, each employee can apply for the visa without the need for the company to qualify further.

For both E-1 and E-2 visas, the employer must be owned by nationals of one of these countries, and the employee must be a national of the same country. For example, the US subsidiary of Sony or Toyota can hire Japanese nationals in E-1 or E-2 status. In addition, the national of the treaty country cannot be a US citizen or permanent resident. If a company is traded on a national stock exchange, it will be deemed to be owned by citizens of that country.

E-1 and E-2 employees are almost identical to L-1 employees. They are either managers or executives, or they are **key employees**. A "key employee" is someone who "possesses skills essential to the firm's operations in the United States," and therefore is similar to (but not the same as) an L-1B employee with "specialized knowledge."

⇨ **Marriage Benefit Tip**   Spouses of E-1 and E-2 employees are eligible to work (unlike spouses of H-1B employees).

B-1 Visitors for Business

Often, a **B-1** visa can be used to visit the US before an H-1B visa is available. Requirements for the B-1 visa include the following:

- The purpose of the visit is for meetings, training, or technology transfer, and not to perform the regular job duties that a US employee (or H-1B employee) would normally perform.

- The US company may not pay the visitor's salary (although it may pay for travel expenses, including food and lodging).

Normally, a B-1 visa will be helpful to a US company that has overseas operations and that may need to transfer employees to the US for short periods to perform permitted B-1 activities (training, liaison, sales calls, meetings, and so forth). During the US visit, the employee remains on the payroll of the foreign operations of the US company. The B-1 visitor must demonstrate that his or her activities in the US will directly benefit the operations, marketing, or revenues of the foreign company.

Visitors for business normally must obtain a B-1 visa from a US embassy or consulate, and those visas are often valid for ten years. However, people from countries that have a **Visa Waiver Program** can visit for up to 90 days without a visa. Like visitors who have visas, those who enter the US using the Visa

Waiver Program should be prepared to convince the immigration inspector that they are coming to the US for bona fide business reasons and not to take up employment in the US.

⇨ **Documentation Tip**   Documents to be submitted when an individual wishes to enter the US as a business visitor might include a letter from the sending company confirming that the visitor will remain on the foreign payroll and explaining how the visit will benefit the company. It can also be helpful to have a letter from the company to be visited that provides a schedule of events and activities in which the visitor will be engaged.

Recently, the US State Department confirmed that it will continue to issue *B-1 in Lieu of H-1* visas, for short-term projects in the US of less than six months. Those projects exceed in complexity and duration the typical activities a business visitor is permitted to engage in (i.e., they can be more than just meetings or training).

Employment Authorization of Students (OPT)

Students in the US in *F-1* status are able to obtain *Practical Training* after completion of their studies (or in some cases while attending college). This "Practical Training" does not have to involve a formal training program, but instead can be regular employment similar to H-1B employment. The "training" aspect of this employment authorization simply means that the work is in the same field as the college studies.

There are two types of Practical Training: **OPT** (*Optional Practical Training*) and **CPT** (*Curricular Practical Training*). CPT is relatively rare and granted through work-study programs, so it is not a very good substitute for H-1B status. We will therefore focus on OPT.

OPT status is normally granted for one year, but that can be extended to 29 months (almost three years!) for those who earned US college degrees in science, technology, engineering, or math (STEM).

OPT status is granted upon graduation from a degree program and can be renewed for another year after completion of each educational level. For example, a STEM student can get 29 months of OPT after completing a bachelor's degree, another 29 months after completing a master's degree, and another 29 months after completing a PhD (for a total of more than seven years in OPT status). However, OPT cannot be granted a second time after the individual has obtained a second degree at the same level. For example, a person who completes a year of OPT after completing a Bachelor's degree in Accounting, cannot get a second round of OPT after completing a Bachelor's degree in Information Systems.

OPT provides a very useful transition to H-1B status and solves the vexing problem of timing the H-1B petition for the quota. The individual can start employment soon after graduation, and the employer can submit the H-1B petition the following April 1, when USCIS begins accepting H-1B petitions for the following fiscal year (see Chapter 3). Even if the OPT would normally expire before the H-1B status begins, USCIS policy extends the F-1 OPT until the following October 1, when the employee can begin working in H-1B status. This policy is called **cap gap relief**.[2]

  # J-1 Visas for Trainees or Interns

Occasionally, an employer will seek a **J-1** visa for a potential employee as a means to avoid problems with the H-1B quota, with the intention of changing that person's status to H-1B status when the quota is open. However, the J-1 regulations indicate that the purpose of the J-1 program is to train professionals for work in their home countries and that a J-1 visa is not to be used as a substitute for H-1B status. So even though you may hear of individuals using the J-1 visa as a means to start employment before an H-1B visa becomes available, a J-1 visa really should be used primarily for training those who will return to work outside of the US.

There is no visa petition for the J-1 visa. Instead, before the trainee applies for the J-1 visa, a recognized program sponsor must accept the trainee and issue a **Form DS-2019**. Many universities and research foundations have become J-1 program sponsors to enable the hiring of professors, researchers, and trainees in their own programs. In addition, some program sponsors will work with employers to secure J-1 status for trainees.[3]

---

[2] This policy is explained on the USCIS website at http://www.uscis.gov/portal/site/uscis/ menuitem.5af9bb95919f35e66f614176543f6d1a/?vgnextoid=1d175ffaae4b7210VgnVCM10000 0082ca60aRCRD&vgnextchannel=6abe6d26d17df110VgnVCM1000004718190aRCRD.

[3] Examples of J-1 program sponsors include American Immigration Council (www. internationalexchangecenter.org), Cultural Vistas (http://culturalvistas.org/host-companies) and the International Exchange Center (www.internationalexchangecenter.org/apply-program). A complete list of approved J-1 sponsors for trainees can be found at http://j1visa. state.gov/participants/how-to-apply/sponsor-search/?program=Trainee.

Caution J-1 visas can disrupt future plans for work in or immigration to the US. If the J-1 program is sponsored with government funds, or if the J-1 visa holder has special skills that are needed in his or her home country, the trainee must return to the home country for two years before applying for an H-1B visa, L-1 visa, or green card.

 # O-1 Visas for People Outstanding in Their Field

Some people are so exceptional that USCIS has created a special **O-1** visa category for them ("O" for "Outstanding"). **Outstanding** is defined as "a level of expertise indicating that the person is one of the small percentage who have arisen to the *very top of the field of endeavor*" in the sciences, education, business, or athletics. There is a significantly lower standard for those in the "arts" (which includes the performing and culinary arts), where the employee must be **prominent**.

The procedure for obtaining the O-1 visa is similar to that for the H-1B visa (but without the LCA and without the quota). A petition is first submitted to USCIS, and if it is approved, the employee will be issued an O-1 visa at a US embassy or consulate abroad.

 # Q-1 Visas for Language and Culture Teachers

Another alternative to an H-1B visa is a **Q-1** visa, which is issued to enable the sharing of the history, culture, and traditions of the employee's home country. This visa can be useful in limited circumstances, such as employment at a primary or secondary school that teaches the language and culture of the home country. A Q-1 visa also might be available to a college teacher (for example, an Indian national teaching about the history or religions of India), but it is not a very useful alternative, since colleges and universities are not subject to the H-1B quota and thus can hire teachers without the constraints imposed by the quota system. Q-1 visa status is granted for a maximum of 15 months.

Summary

Securing your H-1B visa requires attention to both (1) eligibility and (2) H-1B procedures.

H-1B eligibility depends on three essential requirements:

1. The H-1B employee must be a professional with a bachelor's degree in the field or equivalent.

2. The job must be a professional position that normally requires a person with a specialty bachelor's degree or equivalent.

3. The offered salary must be comparable to the salaries paid to American workers.

H-1B procedures required to secure H-1B status involve inputs from both employer and employee in interactions with four different US government agencies:

1. The Labor Condition Application (LCA), filed with the US Department of Labor (DOL).

2. The H-1B petition, filed with US Citizenship and Immigration Services (USCIS).

3. The H-1B visa application, at a US embassy or consulate, the diplomatic posts of the US Department of State (DOS).

4. Application to enter the United States, determined by US Customs and Border Protection (CBP).

H-1B penalties and liabilities result primarily from the employer's failure to pay a sufficient salary and, to a lesser extent, failure to comply with requirements that ensure that a sufficient salary is paid. Those requirements include posting notices at each location of employment. However, penalties may also be assessed against employees for violating H-1B status (for example, by working for another employer without authorization) or for fraud (for example, by submitting a false document).

After the employee secures the H-1B visa, the H-1B status must be maintained by the employer's timely petitioning for renewal before it expires, by successor employers' submitting a new petition with each change of employment, and by the employer's submitting a new LCA (and perhaps a new H-1B petition as well) when the place of employment changes.

There is a time limit on H-1B status (six years), but that limit can be eliminated by starting the process of applying for permanent residence (green card) status before the end of the fifth year in H-1B status.

Initial H-1B petitions (that is, petitions for employees who are not already in H-1B status and who have not been in H-1B status previously) are subject to a quota, so careful advance planning is required for the start of employment. Many employers, such as universities, are exempt from the H-1B quota and can hire new H-1B employees at any time. There are visa alternatives, such as L-1, E, and TN, for those who cannot afford to wait for the quota timetable.

H-1B visas can be the first step to securing US permanent residence status and eventually, if desired, US citizenship (which is available five years after becoming a permanent resident). There are two related reasons why the H-1B visa normally must be used as a stepping stone to US permanent residence. First, the typical permanent residence case takes many years to complete, and H-1B status gives a professional employee the right to live and work in the United States while it is pending. Second, employers normally are unwilling to sponsor green card applications for employees who are not already working for them and proving themselves to be worth the employers' substantial investment in securing green card status.

For employees, the H-1B visa is their gateway to a new life in a new country and perhaps also an opportunity for their descendants to become part of the great melting pot of America. For employers, the H-1B program affords an invaluable means to revitalize their work force, use new talent and new ideas, increase competitiveness, and draw from a worldwide applicant pool of the best and the brightest professional workers.

4-1. *Occupational Outlook Handbook*: Entry for "Computer Support Specialists"[1]

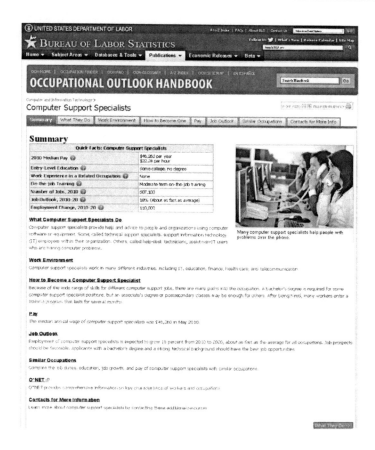

[1] Source: www.bls.gov/ooh/computer-and-information-technology/computer-support-specialists.htm

4-2. *Occupational Outlook Handbook*: Entry for "Software Developers"[2]

5-1. Dual Representation and Conflict of Interest Disclosure Notice and Consent

LAW OFFICES OF JAMES A. BACH
The Shell Building, Nineteenth Floor
100 Bush Street, Suite 1980
San Francisco, CA 94104-3902

(415) 248-3100

Website: www.immilaw.com
Email: jbach@immilaw.com
Facsimile: (415) 248-3105

TO: Employees and Future Employees of ABC, Inc.

FROM: Law Offices of James A. Bach

DUAL REPRESENTATION AND CONFLICT OF INTEREST
DISCLOSURE NOTICE AND CONSENT

Certain immigration matters involving an employer's sponsorship of an employee require my representation on behalf of *both* the employer/sponsor *and* the beneficiary/employee before the U.S. Department of Homeland Security, the U.S. Labor Department, a state employment agency, and the U.S. Department of State. While such dual representation is possible and is the normal practice in such cases, it is possible that a conflict of interest could arise between you and your employer. Rules of professional conduct therefore require that you consent in writing to such representation before it commences.

As I am sure you can imagine, any number of conflicts could arise in an employment situation such as where the employer may want to terminate the employee; the employee may quit; the company could change its ownership, structure or location thereby impacting the underlying requirements for a visa; the employer may wish to transfer you to another position within the company; or you may wish to transfer to another position within the company. Any of these events could affect the employee's right to a particular immigration status. A dispute between an employer and employee or the departure of an employee can cause certain immigration and labor law consequences to the employer or to the employee. Moreover, if an immigration benefit is denied by one of the agencies previously mentioned, there may be a conflict if the employee cannot continue working under state or federal law, or if one party wishes to proceed with an appeal while the other does not. Moreover, if the employee "falls out of status," that employee may be subject to deportation and the employer can be subject to sanctions if the employee remains on the job. The amount of your salary may determine your eligibility for H-1B status or labor certification. These are examples of some conflicts that can arise from the attorney's point of view. If both employer and employee are my clients, you can readily see the difficulty – or impossibility – of fully discharging my duties to either.

At this preliminary stage, we believe our representation of both of you before the various agencies involved does not, in fact, create a conflict of interest. Our policy, however, is to comply strictly with all ethical rules of the State Bar and to avoid any conflict that might diminish the quality of your representation. The State Bar Rules do not prohibit representation of adverse or conflicting interests, but merely require prior disclosure and written consent before such representation may proceed. In addition, an attorney is prohibited from disclosing confidential information without the informed consent of the client.

We suggest that the following procedure be followed to avoid conflicting representation:

Employee's Dual Representation Consent
December 12, 2012
Page 2 of 4

1. For the limited purpose of obtaining immigration benefits, we will *not* be acting as your advisor or advocate with regard to the *terms* of your employment arrangement with ABC, Inc. In separate negotiations with ABC, Inc., you may have already agreed that your employment is to be "at will" (that is, it may be terminated by either you or ABC, Inc. at any time, without notice, and without cause or reason). As ABC, Inc.'s attorney, I will assert this "at will" employment policy in connection with your immigration case. If you desire legal counsel with regard to negotiating your employment arrangement, including details of wages and working conditions, you are free to retain independent legal counsel.

2. Notwithstanding the joint representation exception above, you agree that our legal representation of ABC, Inc. for your benefit does not include disclosure to you of any confidential payroll data or other sources of prevailing wage information, tax returns, income and revenue data, assets and expense data, or other information that ABC, Inc., within reasonable lawful limits, wishes to keep confidential.

3. ABC, Inc. may be required by law to make certain background documentation available to the public or to certain government agencies. If you wish to review this documentation, you will make a request directly to ABC, Inc. without our involvement.

4. Since both you and ABC, Inc. will be our clients there can be no secrets. You should therefore not confide in us any information unless you are prepared to also divulge that information to ABC, Inc. Of course, any information you give to us will remain confidential with respect to third parties (that is, anyone other than the management or attorneys of ABC, Inc.).

5. We will keep confidential from all parties, including your employer, matters relating to serious health conditions and criminal charges, activities, or convictions, and will not disclose such information to any one without your consent.

6. We will keep confidential from you your employer's tax returns, other financial data relating to the company, and personnel plans (including plans to hire, fire, change job duties, or pay), even though it may be relevant to your immigration case.

7. If a conflict of interest should arise, we may withdraw from my representation of you, although we may continue to represent ABC, Inc. in your case as well as other matters. In the alternative, we may obtain your written consent to continue working on the case.

8. If and when you become aware of any fact or development creating a conflict with ABC, Inc., you should inform us immediately, at which time we will either withdraw from our representation of you or obtain your written consent to continue working on the case.

9. If and when it appears that you might benefit through the representation of separate counsel for purposes of other matters, we shall so advise you.

10. Many, if not most, of the immigration-related applications and petitions we will file in connection with your case are signed by the company. Nonimmigrant visa petitions such as H-1, L-1 and O-1 petitions, and immigrant visa petitions based on employment (I-140) are solely the employer's petition, even though they affect and benefit you. The labor certification application is signed and submitted jointly by you *and*

the employer. By signing below, you agree that our law firm can amend or withdraw such petitions and applications at the request of ABC, Inc. without your knowledge and consent. We will not amend or withdraw applications signed and submitted solely by you (such as the application for adjustment of status or an application for an Employment Authorization Document) without your knowledge and consent. We may however amend or withdraw such an application if we believe it is in your best interest and it is impractical to obtain your knowledge and consent, or if the amendment or withdrawal is a minor or procedural matter. Although we will not amend or withdraw against your interest applications signed solely by you, we may withdraw as attorney as indicated above.

By using the above procedures, we can avoid potential conflicts of interest without sacrificing the benefits of common representation. By agreeing that we should proceed with the case, you agree to this dual representation and the conditions of our representation set forth above.

We will provide you with a copy of relevant documents as the case progress, but once the case is concluded we will retain your file for at least three years and then shred it to protect your confidential information. No additional notice will be given before destruction of your file. By signing below, you acknowledge this practice and consent to the later destruction of your file without further notice.

In addition, by signing this consent form, you agree that you are not aware of any existing interest you have in this matter that conflicts with that of ABC, Inc.

If you have any questions or comments, or have any information pertaining to a possible conflict, please contact us immediately.

If you wish for us to continue the representation, please sign the consent form below and return this entire memorandum to my office, retaining a copy for your records. Please note that we must receive a signed copy of this consent form before we can give you any advice or take any further action in your case.

CONSENT

I have read and understood this memorandum and I understand the potential conflicts of interest outlined above. I voluntarily and freely consent to dual representation in this matter by the Law Offices of James A. Bach. I consent to the destruction of my file at least three years after the representation has ended.

_____
(Signature)

_____
(Date)

6-1. AAO Processing Times as of October 1, 2012[1]

Form Number	Case Type	Time
I-129CW	CNMI-Only Nonimmigrant Transitional Worker	Current
I-129F	Petition for Fiancée	Current
I-129 H1B	Nonimmigrant Specialty Occupation Worker	12 Months
I-129 H2	Temporary Nonimmigrant Worker	Current
I-129 H3	Temporary Nonimmigrant Trainee	Current
I-129 L	Nonimmigrant Intracompany Transferee	13 Months
I-129 O	Nonimmigrant Extraordinary Ability Worker	Current
I-129 P1, P2, P3	Athletes, Artists and Entertainers	Current
I-129 Q	Cultural Exchange Worker	Current
I-129 R	Nonimmigrant Religious Worker	Current
I-131	Application for Travel Document	Current
I-140 EB1	(A) Alien with Extraordinary Ability	Current
I-140 EB1	(B) Outstanding Professor or Researcher	Current
I-140 EB1	(C) Multinational Manager or Executive	13 Months
I-140 EB2	(D) Advanced Degree Professional	7 Months

[1] www.uscis.gov/portal/site/uscis/menuitem.5af9bb95919f35e66f614176543f6d1a/?vgnextoid=8ff31eeaf28e6210VgnVCM100000082ca60aRCRD&vgnextchannel=dfe316685e1e6210VgnVCM100000082ca60aRCRD

I-140 EB2	(I) National Interest Waiver	Current
I-140 EB3	(E) Skilled or Professional Worker	29 Months
I-140 EB3	(G) Other Worker	Current
I-212	Application to Reapply for Admission	Current
I-352	Bond Breach	Current
I-360 EB4	Petition for Religious Worker	Current
I-360 A	Amerasian	Current
I-360 C	Special Immigrant Juvenile	Current
I-360 K	Special Immigrant Afghanistan or Iraq National Translator	Current
I-360 VAWA	Violence Against Women Act Petition	Current
I-360 E	Special Immigrant Canal Zone	Current
I-360 F	Special Immigrant Physican	Current
I-360 H	Special Immigrant Armed Forces Member	Current
I-360 G	Special Immigrant Intl Org. Employee	Current
I-360 L	Special Immigrant Iraq National US Employee	Current
I-360 M	Special Immigrant Other	Current
I-485	Cuban Adjustment Act Application	Current
I-485 LIFE	LIFE Act Adjustment Application	Current
I-485 Dplmt	Section 13 Adjustment Application	Current
I-485 T	T Visa Nonimmigrant Adjustment	Current
I-485 U	U Visa Nonimmigrant Adjustment	Current
I-526 EB5	Alien Entrepreneur	Current
I-600	Petition for Orphan	Current
I-601	Application for Waiver of Inadmissibility	17 Months
I-612	Application for 212(e) Waiver	Current
I-687	Legalization Application for Temporary Residence	Current
I-690	Legalization/SAW -Waive Grounds of Excludability	Current
I-698	Legalization Adjustment Application	Current

I-700	Special Agricultural Worker	Current
I-821	Temporary Protected Status	Current
I-800	Convention Adoption as an Immediate Relative	Current
I-905	Application to Issue Cert for Health Care Workers	Current
I-914	Application for T Nonimmigrant Status	Current
I-918	Petition for U Nonimmigrant Status	Current
I-924	Application for Regional Center	Current
I-929	Qualifying Family Member of a U Nonimmigrant	Current
N-470	Application to Preserve Residence	Current
N-565	Replacement Naturalization/Citizenship Doc	Current
N-600	Certificate of Citizenship	Current
N-643	Certificate of Citizenship for Adopted Child	Current

* Within current USCIS processing time goal of six months or less

APPENDIX

8

8-1. Specific Vocational Preparation (SVP)[1]

Specific Vocational Preparation is defined as the amount of lapsed time required by a typical worker to learn the techniques, acquire the information, and develop the facility needed for average performance in a specific job-worker situation.

This training may be acquired in a school, work, military, institutional, or vocational environment. It does not include the orientation time required of a fully qualified worker to become accustomed to the special conditions of any new job. Specific vocational training includes: vocational education, apprenticeship training, in-plant training, on-the- job training, and essential experience in other jobs.

Specific vocational training includes training given in any of the following circumstances:

a. Vocational education (high school; commercial or shop training; technical school; art school; and that part of college training which is organized around a specific vocational objective);

b. Apprenticeship training (for apprenticeable jobs only);

c. In-plant training (organized classroom study provided by an employer);

d. On-the-job training (serving as learner or trainee on the job under the instruction of a qualified worker);

e. Essential experience in other jobs (serving in less responsible jobs which lead to the higher grade job or serving in other jobs which qualify).

[1] Source: Appendix E in *Prevailing Wage Determination Policy Guidance* (Employment and Training Administration, Revised November 2009), www.foreignlaborcert.doleta.gov/pdf/NPWHC_Guidance_Revised_11_2009.pdf.

The following is an explanation of the various levels of specific vocational preparation:

Level	Time
1	Short demonstration only
2	Anything beyond short demonstration up to and including 1 month
3	Over 1 month up to and including 3 months
4	Over 3 months up to and including 6 months
5	Over 6 months up to and including 1 year
6	Over 1 year up to and including 2 years
7	Over 2 years up to and including 4 years
8	Over 4 years up to and including 10 years
9	Over 10 years

Note: The levels of this scale are mutually exclusive and do not overlap.

8-2. OES Prevailing Wage Guidance[2]

All employer applications for a prevailing wage determination shall initially be considered an entry level or Level I wage. The employer's requirements for experience, education, training, and special skills shall be compared to those generally required furan occupation as described in O*NET and shall be used as indicators that the job opportunity is for an experienced (Level II), qualified (Level III), or fully competent (Level IV) worker and warrants a prevailing wage determination at a higher wage level.

All prevailing wage determinations start with a Level I determination; therefore, the check sheet and worksheet have a 1 entered in the Wage Level Column.

Step 1 - Enter the O*NET Requirements on the Worksheet

- Use the O*NET OnLine 'Find Occupations' feature (http://online.onetcenter.org)to determine the appropriate O*NET-

---

[2] Source: Appendix A in *Prevailing Wage Determination Policy Guidance*.

SOC code based on the job title provided on the prevailing wage determination request form.

- Enter the job title from the employer's job offer into the Quick Search box and click on Go.

- Select the O*NET occupation that most closely matches the employer's request from the resulting list of occupations.

- Review the Tasks, Knowledge, Work Activities, and Job Zone information contained in the O*NET summary report to gain an understanding of what is generally required for vocational preparation and performance in that occupation.

Enter the O*NET education and experience requirements on the Worksheet.

Step 2 - Complete the Experience Section of the Worksheet

Compare the overall experience described in the O*NET Job Zone to the years of experience required by the employer on the prevailing wage determination request form.

For occupations contained in Job Zone 1, if the employer's experience requirement is equivalent to that described in an:

- SVP of 1 (experience requirement of a short duration), enter a 0 in the Wage Level Column.

- SVP of 2 (experience requirement of anything beyond short duration and up to 1 month), enter a 1 in the Wage Level Column.

- SVP of 3 (experience requirement of over 1 month up to and including 3 months), enter a 2 in the Wage Level Column.

- SVP of 4 (experience requirement of over 3 months up to and including 6 months), enter a 3 in the Wage Level Column.

Refer to Appendix E: Specific Vocational Preparation (SVP) for an explanation of the experience requirements related to an SVP level.

For occupations in Job Zones 2 through 5, if the employer's experience requirement is:

- At or below the level of experience and SVP range, make no entry in the Wage Level Column.

- In the low end of the experience and SVP range, enter a 1 in the Wage Level Column.

- In the high end of the experience and SVP range, enter a 2 in the Wage Level Column.

- Greater than the experience and SVP range, enter a 3 in the Wage Level Column.

Points should be added for the amount of experience only if the required work experience is above the starting point of the O*NET job zone range. *Education required for the job is addressed in Step 3 of the worksheet, and therefore the years of education required should not be considered in Step 2. However, if education is considered as an equivalent amount of experience in Step 2, it should not also be considered in Step 3.*

Step 3 - Complete the Education Section of the Worksheet

Compare the education requirement generally required for an occupation to the education requirement in the employer's job offer.

Determine if the level required by the employer's job offer is greater than what is generally required.

Professional Occupations by O*NET-SOC category and the related education and training category code are listed in Appendix A to the Preamble of the PERM regulations. The education and training categories assigned to those occupations shall be considered the usual education and training required when considering the education level for prevailing wage determinations. A listing of occupations designated as professional occupations and the related education and training category can be found in Appendix D of this document.

For professional occupations:

- If the education required on the prevailing wage determination request form is equal to or less than the usual education contained in Appendix D, make no entry in the Wage Level Column.

- If the education required on the prevailing wage determination request form is more than the usual education contained in Appendix D by one category, enter a 1 on the worksheet in the Wage Level Column.

- If the education required is more than the usual education contained in Appendix D by more than one category, enter a 2 on the worksheet in the Wage Level Column.

Example: If the occupation generally requires a Bachelor's degree and the employer's job offer requires a Master's degree, enter a 1; if the job offer requires a Ph.D., enter a 2.

For all other occupations, use the education level for what 'most of these occupations' require or 'these occupations usually require' described in the O*NET Job Zone for that occupation.

- If the education or training is equal to or less than what 'most occupations require' or the level that these occupations 'usually' require, make no entry in the Wage Level Column.

- If the education or training is more than what 'most occupations require' or the level that these occupations 'usually' require, enter a 1 on the worksheet in the Wage Level Column.

- If the education or training required on the prevailing wage determination request form is more than the level described by what 'some may require,' enter a 2 on the worksheet in the Wage Column.

Experience required for the job is addressed in Step 2 of the worksheet, and therefore the years of experience required should not be considered in Step 3.

Step 4 - Complete the Special Skills and Other Requirements Section of the Worksheet

- Review the job title, job description (duties), and special requirements on the prevailing wage determination request form to identify the tasks, work activities, knowledge, and skills required. An employer's requirement for an occupational license and/or certification should be evaluated to determine if they are indicators of a requirement for special skills warranting the award of a point or points on the worksheet. They may not necessarily be such an indicator.

- Make note of machines, equipment, tools, or computer software used. Consider how the employer's requirements compare to the O*NET Tasks, Work Activities, Knowledge, and Job Zone Examples. Consider whether the employer's requirements indicate the need for skills beyond those of an entry-level worker.

- In situations where the employer's requirements are not listed in the O*NET Tasks, Work Activities, Knowledge, and Job Zone Examples for the selected occupation, then the requirements should be evaluated to determine if they represent special skills. The requirement of a specific skill not listed in the O*NET does not necessitate that a point be added. If the specific skills required for the job are generally encompassed by the O*NET description for the position, no point should be added. However, if it is determined that the requirements are indicators of skills that are beyond those of an entry level worker, consider whether a point should be entered on the worksheet in the Wage Level Column.

Note: A language requirement other than English in an employer's job offer shall generally be considered a special skill for all occupations, with the exception of Foreign Language Teachers and Instructors, Interpreters, and Caption Writers, and a point should be entered on the worksheet.

It is recognized, however, that there may be circumstances where a foreign language is required for the job, but that requirement does not sufficiently increase the seniority and complexity of the position such that a point must be added for the foreign language requirement (e.g. Specialty Cooks).

- If the employer's job opportunity requires the possession of a license or certification, the NPWHC must give careful consideration to the occupation in question and the education, training, and experience requirements of the license or certification to evaluate whether possession of a license or certification is an indicator that the offer of employment is for an experienced worker.

- An employer's requirement for the possession of an occupational license or certification does not constitute a situation where a point must automatically be awarded. The NPWHC should look at the employer's job description and stated requirements to evaluate, along with other factors, whether the position is closely supervised, involves only moderately complex duties, and allows limited exercise of independent judgment. If the license or certification is a normal requirement to perform the job duties as an entry level worker, no point should be added on the worksheet in the Wage Column, e.g., attorney, teacher, registered nurse.

- Some occupations have more than one license and the requirements of the license provide an indicator of the level of independent judgment and complexity of tasks required of the licensee, e.g. Journeyman Plumber or Master Plumber. The NPWHC must consider the education, training and experience requirements of the license or certification to determine when points should be entered on the worksheet in the Wage Column.

If a substantial amount of work experience, education or training is required to obtain a license or certification and this results in the total amount of necessary work experience being on the high end of the O*NET job zone range, a point could be added either in Step 2 for the work experience, or Step 3 for the education or training, or in Step 4 for the license. A point or points should not be added in every step.

Step 5 - Complete the Supervisory Duties Section of the Worksheet

- Review the prevailing wage determination request form to determine the number or range of people to be supervised to determine if there is a supervisory requirement; and

- If the number is greater than 0, then enter a 1 on the worksheet in the Wage Level Column.

Exception: If supervision is a customary duty for the O*NET occupation (e.g., First-line Supervisors/Managers occupations), do not enter a 1 on the worksheet in the Wage Level Column.

Note: Previous guidance suggested that an employer's job offer that included supervisory duties should be assigned the higher of the two previous wage levels. In this new guidance, an employer's job requirement for supervisory duties will not automatically warrant a determination of the highest wage level because the wages for supervisory occupations already account for the supervision of employees. The guidance contained above for evaluating education, experience, and skills required in an employer's job offer should be used to determine the appropriate wage level for supervisory occupations.

Determine the wage level by summing the numbers in the Wage Level Column of the worksheet. The sum total shall equal the wage for the prevailing wage determination. If the sum total is greater than 4, then the wage level shall be Level 4.

The process described above should not be implemented in an automated fashion. The NPWHC must exercise judgment when making prevailing wage determinations. The wage level should be commensurate with the complexity of tasks, independent judgment required, and amount of close supervision received as described in the employer's job opportunity.

8-3. Worksheet for Use in Determining OES Wage Level[3]

Employer's Job Title:

O*NET Title: Date:

O*NET Code: Reviewer:

Indicator	Job Offer Requirements	O*NET- Usual Require- ments	Com- ments	Wage Level Result
Step 1. Requirements				
Step 2. Experience				
Step 3. Education				
Step 4. Special Skills and Other Requirements? (Y/N)				
Step 5. Supervisory duties (Y/N)				
			Sum:	

---

[3] Source: Appendix C in *Prevailing Wage Determination Policy Guidance.*

8-4. DOL Guidance for Private Surveys[4]

Wage Determinations Using Employer Provided Wage Surveys

If the job opportunity is in an occupation not covered by a collective bargaining agreement, the NPWHC shall also consider wage data that has been furnished by the employer; i.e., wage data contained in a published wage survey that has been provided by the employer, or wage data contained in a survey that has been conducted or funded by the employer.

. . . The use of such employer provided wage data is an employer option. However, in each case where the employer submits wage data for consideration, it will be incumbent upon the employer to make a written showing that the survey or other wage data meet the criteria outlined below. The employer must provide the NPWHC with enough information about the survey methodology (e.g., sample size and source, sample selection procedures, survey job descriptions) to allow the NPWHC to make a determination with regard to the adequacy of the data provided and the validity of the statistical methodology used in conducting the survey.

Criteria for Employer Provided Surveys

(1) The survey must be recent.

If the employer submits a published survey, that survey must:

- have been published within 24 months of the date of submission of the prevailing wage request;
- be the most current edition of the survey; and
- be based on data collected within 24 months of the date of the publication of the survey.

If the employer submits a survey conducted by the employer, the survey must be based on data collected within 24 months of the date of submission of the prevailing wage request.

(2) The wage data submitted by the employer must reflect the area of intended employment.

Area of intended employment means the area within normal commuting distance of the place (address) of intended employment.

---

[4] Source: Section C (pp. 14-16) in *Prevailing Wage Determination Policy Guidance*.

- If the place of intended employment is within a Metropolitan Statistical Area (MSA) or Primary Metropolitan Statistical Area (PMSA), any place within the MSA or PMSA is deemed to be within the normal commuting distance of the place of intended employment.

- All locations within a Consolidated Metropolitan Statistical Area (CMSA) will not automatically be deemed to be within normal commuting distances for prevailing wage purposes.

- The borders of PMSAs, MSAs, or CMSAs are not controlling in the identification of the normal commuting area; an employer location just outside of the PMSA, MSA, or CMSA boundary may still be considered within normal commuting distance.

The terminology CMSAs and PMSAs are being replaced by the Office of Management and Budget (OMB); however, ETA will continue to recognize the use of these area concepts as well as their replacements.

(3) The job description applicable to wage data submitted by the employer must be adequate to determine that the data represents workers who are similarly employed. Similarly employed means jobs requiring substantially similar levels of skills.

(4) The wage data must have been collected across industries that employ workers in the occupation.

(5) The prevailing wage determination should be based on the arithmetic mean (weighted average) of wages for workers that are similarly employed in the area of intended employment. If the survey provides a median wage of workers similarly employed in the area of intended employment and does not provide an arithmetic mean, the median wage shall be used as the basis for making a prevailing wage determination.

(6) In all cases where an employer provides the NPWHC with wage data for which it seeks acceptance, the employer must include the methodology used for the survey to show that it is reasonable and consistent with recognized statistical standards and principles in producing a prevailing wage (e.g., contains a representative sample), including its adherence to these standards for the acceptability of employer provided wage data. It is important to note that a prevailing wage determination based upon the acceptance of employer provided wage data for the specific job opportunity at issue does not supersede the OES wage rate for subsequent requests for prevailing wage data in that occupation.

Information from employers that consists merely of speculation, subjective impressions, or pleas that it cannot afford to pay the prevailing wage rate determined by the NPWHC will not be taken into consideration in making a wage determination. If the NPWHC does not find the employer provided wage survey acceptable, the NPWHC must notify the employer in writing and include the reasons the survey was not found to be acceptable. Upon receiving this determination, the employer may provide supplemental information, file a new request, or appeal the determination.

In issuing wage determinations, the NPWHC may be required to convert an hourly rate to a weekly, monthly, or annual rate, or to convert a weekly, monthly, or annual rate to an hourly rate. As a matter of policy, such conversions shall be based on 2,080 hours of work in a year.

Factors relating to the nature of the employer, such as whether the employer is public or private, for profit or nonprofit, large or small, charitable, a religious institution, a job contractor, or a struggling or prosperous firm, do not bear in a significant way on the skills and knowledge levels required and, therefore, are not relevant to determining the prevailing wage for an occupation under the regulations at 20 CFR 655.10 and 20 CFR 656.40. As noted above, the relevant factors are the job, the geographic locality of the job, and the level of skill required to perform independently on the job.

9-1. Audit Letter

U.S. Department of Labor	Wage and Hour Division
	90 7th Street, Suite #18-300
	San Francisco, CA 94103
	Phone: (415) 625-7727
	Fax: (415) 625-7735

June 27, 2011

Dear Mr. and Ms. ▮▮▮▮

This is to advise you that ▮▮▮▮▮▮▮▮ Inc has been scheduled for a review to determine compliance with Regulations Part 655, Labor Condition Applications and Requirements for Employers Using Nonimmigrants on H-1B Visas in Specialty Occupations and Fashion Models. Regulations Part 655 covers the minimum wages, recordkeeping, and other laws directly related to non-immigrants employed in the United States under the H1B Visa provisions. The authority for this review is contained in Regulations Part 655.

In addition to being available for questions regarding ▮▮▮▮▮▮▮▮ Inc., please have the following documents and information available at your establishment in order to conduct a timely review:

1. Payroll records for all current and former employees employed from **June 27, 2009 through June 26, 2011** working in and reporting to the US offices. For our purposes, please provide individual earnings records which show the name of each employee, their gross amount paid for each pay period, hours worked daily and weekly individually, and rates of pay. If you do not have individual earnings records, your basic payroll register or check stubs will suffice;

2. Corresponding time records for all current and former employees employed from **June 27, 2009 through June 26, 2011**;

3. Federal Tax I. D. Number;

4. Legal name of the business and officers, partners or owners;

5. Date the company opened for business;

6. If your company is a corporation, the name of the corporation and when it was incorporated;

7. List of all branches, *if any*;

8. *In the event of a change in corporate structure*:

a. Sworn statement by successor entity accepting all liabilities of predecessor entity;
b. List of H-1B workers transferred to successor entity;
c. Each affected LCA number and effective date;
d. Successor entity's actual wage computations; and;
e. Successor entity's employer identification number.

9. A list of entities included as "single employer;"

10. *For H-1B dependent and/or willful violator employers*:

a. List of exempt H-1B workers(s);
b. A summary of recruitment methods used and the time frames of the recruitment of U.S. workers; and;
c. Documentation to show the manner used to demonstrate compliance with the non-displacement obligation (whether direct or indirect).

11. All the Labor Condition Applications Form ETA (LCA - Form ETA 9035 and/or ETA 3035E) submitted to the U.S. Department of Labor Employment and Training Administration (ETA) by your firm for the employment for H-1B workers during the period of **June 4, 2010 through June 3, 2011**;

12. Documentation of the wage rate to be paid to the H-1B worker;

13. A full, clear explanation of the system used to set the actual wage you paid for all occupations in which the H-1B workers were paid during **June 4, 2010 through June 3, 2011**;

14. The documentation used to establish the prevailing wage for all occupations and all areas of employment in which the H-1B workers were employed during **June 4, 2010 through June 3, 2011**;

15. A copy of the document(s) used to satisfy the notification requirements with respect to the employment of the H-1B workers;

16. The names, job titles, and contact information (address, phone numbers, email) of all H1B workers you employed from **June 4, 2010 through June 3, 2011**; and:

a. The Labor Condition Applications (LCA - Form ETA 9035) that was included as part of the H-1B visa application;
b. Resumes for all H1B employees;
c. Salary history of all H1B workers from the date of their initial employment through **June 3, 2011**;
d. An explanation of the deductions made from their weekly wages or any unpaid periods including any supporting documents (i.e. vacation requests, personnel memos, written authorizations for loans or salary advances, etc.);
e. Each worksite where the work was performed each week (Site, City, State) and the period of employment at each site;
f. The date of entry into the U.S.;
g. The date of hire/termination;
h. The date the work commenced;
i. Benefit plans offered and provided to each H-1B worker;
j. Copies of any termination notices to U.S. Citizenship Immigration Services (USCIS) and the USCIS response;
k. A copy of each Petition for Nonimmigrant Worker (Form I-129 and H Supplement) and subsequent USCIS Approval Form (I-797) for each H-1B worker employed during **June 4, 2010 through June 3, 2011**;

    l. Copies of all correspondences sent to and received from the USCIS and all other government entities/agencies relative to all of the status of the H1B workers. (i.e. employment and termination letters) from the date of their employment <u>June 3, 2011</u>; and;

    m. Any liquidation damages or penalties sought or collected from H-1B workers, including relevant contracts, demands, lawsuits, and settlement agreements.

17. Names, job titles, phone numbers and addresses of all US workers employed in the same capacity as the H1B workers employed from <u>June 4, 2010 through June 3, 2011</u>;

18. Summary of benefits offered to U.S. Workers in the same occupations as the H-1B workers;

19. Evidence that Labor Condition Applications were posted to include when and where; and;

20. Public Access File.

Additional information may be requested during the course of the investigation; hence, this list may not be all inclusive.

The inspection of these records is authorized under 20 Code of Federal Regulations, Part 655.760. Whenever such records are maintained at a record-keeping facility distinct from the place of employment, the records must be produced within **72 hours** following notice for their production.

Thank you for your prompt attention to this matter. If you have any questions, please do not hesitate to call me at the phone number above.

Sincerely,

Investigator

10

10-1. Efren Hernandez Letter on When Amended H-1B is Required

U.S. Department of Homeland Security
Citizenship and Immigration Services

425 I Street NW
ULLICO. 3ʳᵈ Floor
Washington, D.C. 20536

October 23, 2003

Ms. Lynn Shotwell
American Council on International Personnel, Inc.
515 Madison Avenue, 6th Floor
New York, NY 10022

Dear Ms. Shotwell:

We regret the delay in responding to your July 12 letter regarding the requirements for filing an amended petition when an H-1B employee transfers to a new location not included on the original Form I-129, but which is covered by a labor condition application (LCA) that was in place prior to the employee's move.

Based on the information you provided, an amended Form I-129 petition would not be required simply on the basis of the geographic move. As long as the LCA has been filed and certified for the new employment location, the appropriate worksite posting has taken place, and other wage and hour obligations are met, no amended petition would be required regardless of when the LCA was filed and certified, as long as the certification took place before the employee was moved. Please note, however, that if any other change takes place that constitutes a material change in the terms and conditions of employment and that affects the beneficiary's eligibility for H-1B classification, an amended petition would be required.

Please also note, as discussed in a legacy INS correspondence, that the U.S. Citizenship and Immigration Services (USCIS) does not encourage "speculative employment," and the better practice would be for employers to include alternative locations in itineraries filed with the original Form I-129 petition if they are planning to move employees. Note that the itineraries must he reflected in a multiple location LCA or multiple LCAs that have already been appropriately posted and certified. The USCIS must be apprised of the move when the subsequent LCA is filed with a request for an extension. Additionally, in all instances, foreign nationals who change their place of residence must comply with immigration regulations pertaining to filing changes of address on Form AR-11 and special registration, if applicable.

Ms. Lynn Shotwell
Page 2

Please be aware that the USCIS will explore the issue of the need to file amended H-1B petitions in the context of regulations implementing the American Competitiveness in the Twenty-First Century Act (AC21), and related legislation. Our position on this issue, therefore, is subject to change.

We hope that this information has been useful to you. If you have further questions concerning this matter, please do not hesitate to contact this office at the above address.

Sincerely,

Efren Hernandez III
Director, Business and Trade Branch

Index

CPSIA information can be obtained at www.ICGtesting.com
Printed in the USA
LVOW051954220113

316782LV00004B/482/P